With a transparency that is at times unsettling, Bill
Hendricks allows the reader to see the way through death's
dark abyss to "the light that never dies."
　　　　　—Joseph M. Stowell, teaching pastor,
　　　　　　Harvest Bible Chapel

Bill's story will leave you with the calm assurance that
God's grace will be there in your time of need.
　　　　　—Andy Stanley, pastor,
　　　　　　North Point Community Church

The Light That Never Dies is profound, intelligent, well-
expressed and reflects a balance of faith that is exceedingly
refreshing. This truth is not only for those who have experienced the death of a loved one, but for all those who
struggle with the security of God's love in the midst of
challenging circumstances.
　　　　　—Marilyn Meberg,
　　　　　　"Women of Faith"

These "words of life" were forged in the furnace of adversity.
The power and light that will lift your soul from this book
merge the rare combination of intellectual honesty and
clear theological thinking poured through a broken heart.
You'll be glad you read it.
　　　　　—Chip Ingram, CEO and president,
　　　　　　Walk Thru the Bible, teaching pastor,
　　　　　　Living on the Edge radio

Grief, struggle, pain, honest questions, hard reality. Bill Hendricks can help anyone as they move forward in journeys of their own.

—Robert Lewis, pastor and author,
The Church of Irresistible Influence

The Light that Never Dies provides comfort and calm for those staggering through the disordered equilibrium that characterizes profound grief.

—William R. Cutrer M.D., director,
A Woman's Choice Resource Center,
Louisville, Kentucky

In this book, ordinary people will find answers to the horrible questions which suffering shouts in our ears. The shape and language of these reflections will touch your heart, open your mind, and deepen the reservoir of your faith for whatever life brings you.

—William L. Murdoch, rector,
All Saints' Church

Bill reveals the beauty, depth, and sufficiency of God's lovingkindness. If you are in the midst of a trial or are desperately in need of hope, this is a must read.

—Mario Zandstra, president and CEO,
Pine Cove Camps

The Light
That Never Dies

*A Story of Hope
in the Shadows of Grief*

WILLIAM
HENDRICKS

NORTHFIELD PUBLISHING
CHICAGO

All Scripture quotations, unless otherwise indicated, are taken from the *New American Standard Bible®*, Copyright © The Lockman Foundation 1960, 1962, 1963, 1968, 1971, 1972, 1973, 1975, 1977, 1995. Used by permission.

Scripture quotations marked NIV are taken from the *Holy Bible, New International Version®*. NIV®. Copyright © 1973, 1978, 1984 by International Bible Society. Used by permission of Zondervan Publishing House. All rights reserved.

Cover Design: Paetzold Associates
Cover Photo: Getty Images
Interior Design: BlueFrog Design

ISBN: 1-881273-69-5
EAN/ISBN-13: 978-1-881273-69-1

Library of Congress Cataloging-in-Publication Data

Hendricks, William, 1954-
   The light that never dies : a story of hope in the shadows of grief /
William Hendricks.
      p. cm.
   Includes bibliographical references.
   ISBN-13: 978-1-881273-69-1
   1. Consolation. I. Title.

BV4905.3.H46 2005
248.8'6—dc22

2004023582

1 3 5 7 9 10 8 6 4 2

Printed in the United States of America

This book is dedicated to Nancy, as it must be,
and to the three she gave to me and to the world,
and to Ann Kathryn,
the little angel who inspired me to write it.

About the Author

WILLIAM HENDRICKS (B.A., Harvard University; M.A., Boston University; M.A., Dallas Theological Seminary) is president of The Giftedness Center, a Dallas-based consulting firm specializing in organizational design and strategic people management (www.thegiftednesscenter.com). Bill is the author or coauthor of a dozen books, including the classic *Your Work Matters to God, Living by the Book,* and most recently, *The Power of Uniqueness.* His writings have appeared in *The Wall Street Journal, The Dallas Morning News, Christianity Today,* and numerous other publications. He is the proud father of three daughters by his late wife, Nancy.

Kristin, Nancy, Amy, Bill and Brittany Hendricks, July 1998.
Photo courtesy of Richard Michael Pruitt/*Dallas Morning News.*

Contents

ONE

The Intruder
at the Party

I don't think I was asking for much. At thirty-nine, all I wanted was what everybody else seems to want: a healthy, happy family and a job that pays well and proves satisfying. That's it. I wasn't looking to get rich. I wasn't jockeying for power. I wasn't out to make the world bow down at my feet through fame or notoriety.

I simply wanted to get better at loving and living with the woman I had married nearly sixteen years before, the woman who had borne three precocious daughters. We were a healthy, happy family. We were a family of five strong-willed strivers—and the world was our oyster.

As for work, I had made a concerted effort in my twenties to figure out what things fit me, and I was choosing my pursuits accordingly. Consequently, I loved nearly everything I got into. Now, ever curious and ever adventurous, I could hardly wait to see what adventures heaven might send my way as I came to my fourth decade of life.

In short, I was on a quest to live life to the fullest. Not so much in material terms. Oh, I enjoy fine and expensive things as much as the next person. But I've always been driven toward something deeper. I guess you could call it wisdom—the knowing that comes by *experiencing* life and then taking to heart what you have been through.

Part of what made the experience so macabre was the very beauty of everyday life.

In the end, though, it didn't matter whether or not I was born to search out the meaning of life. Because at thirty-nine the search for the meaning of life came searching for me. You see, I spent my midlife watching my wife die. Six weeks after I turned thirty-nine, in November 1993, Nancy was diagnosed with intraductile breast cancer. Seven years after that, in October 2000, she died. Now, having had four years to recover and reflect, I find myself at fifty.

Some midlife, huh? It was a particularly odd position to be in, given the times. Remember the '90s? What a giddy era that was in America. We were patting ourselves on the back for winning the Cold War. We were all gaga over a so-called New Economy that could make billionaires of us all— overnight! And at the end of the decade, we couldn't wait to embrace a bold new century.

It felt to me as if the whole world was throwing itself a party just outside my family's door. Meanwhile, inside our door, I was tasked with watching Nancy die. It was kind of surreal, really.

Not like our home was morbid or glum or uninviting—quite the opposite, most of the time. Indeed, part of what made the experience so macabre was the very beauty of everyday life. The shouts of children running through the yard. The routine of bringing in the mail. Shaking our heads upon finding that long-lost mitten hibernating under a bed. Cleaning up the pee from a new puppy.

It was a home, like any other. Yet not like any other. Nothing is ordinary when every moment, even the simplest of them—and especially the happiest of them—is lived out in the shadow of death. Not always consciously or openly. But unmistakably, there's an awareness that every moment is fleeting.

HOME ALONE

As those moments slipped by, I experienced the truth of an ancient proverb that says,

> It is better to go to a house of mourning
> Than to go to a house of feasting,
> Because that is the end of every man,
> And the living takes it to heart.[1]

A rather jolting statement, isn't it? "Better to go to a house of mourning." Really? *Better?*

I don't know many people who would agree with that. Aren't we all looking to end up in the House of Feasting? To gather with friends, to eat and laugh and celebrate good fortune? Those were certainly my plans ten years ago.

Somehow God had different plans. For reasons known only to Him, the particular limo that Nancy and I were taking to the ball dropped us off at a rather different location. And so we missed the party.

Interesting thing, though. There were quite a few others at the House of Mourning—although I didn't realize it at the time. At the time, Nancy and I felt very lonely there.

That's not to discount the overwhelming support we had from countless people. For example, the group of women— Ellie, Michelle, Nancy, Lyn, Leslie (and others I'm probably forgetting or am unaware of)—who gathered every Thursday night for about four years to pray over, for, and with Nancy.

There was the community group from our church, organized by Melissa and Elaine, who took turns bringing meals anywhere from two to five nights a week for more than two and a half years.

There were families, and especially mothers, in our community who more or less adopted our girls on an as-needed basis. There were doctors and nurses and other medical personnel, pastors, youth workers, teachers, coaches, friends old and new, family, even people I never knew about who came alongside us in ways I don't even know about throughout the whole decade. We were unbelievably blessed with caring, concerned people.

Yet affirming that, and grateful beyond words for those God-sent comforters, let me say again: Nancy and I felt very lonely in the House of Mourning. That's just the way it is there. It doesn't matter how many or how few supporters you have around you. Everyone experiences their suffering as unique to them. And by oneself. Suffering is an a cappella solo.

I remember the day Nancy partici-
pated in a Race for the Cure event at a
mall near our house. (The Susan B.
Komen Foundation sponsors Race for
the Cure to raise money for the fight
against breast cancer.) Nancy and a couple of her friends walked together to celebrate her second year of survival after her
initial diagnosis.

"I don't care about being brave! I just want to see my girls grow up!"

When she came home, I figured she would be elated by the thousands of people who had shown up to cheer for her and other survivors of that dreaded disease. Instead she was in a funk.

"What's the matter?" I asked.

"Everyone kept telling me I'm so brave," she replied. That sounded like a good thing to me. Then my brave sur-vivor broke into tears and blurted out with an edge of anger, "I don't care about being brave! I just want to see my girls grow up!"

Yes, the situation looks completely different when you're inside the dying body than outside it. No one perceives the reality of what's going on quite the way you do. They simply can't, however much they try. I think that's one of the more insidious sides of suffering. Others may be able to see *that* you are in pain, but they can never *have* your exact experi-ence of pain, because pain is about what matters to you, and what matters to you is unique to you.

I experienced a similar loneliness whenever I had to tell

someone about Nancy's situation. For instance, I'd have lunch with a person and they would innocently ask, "So, Bill, tell me about your family."

"Well, my wife and I have three daughters," I'd begin, and we'd talk about the girls. But inevitably we'd get to the part I knew was coming and always hated.

"So, I guess your wife is pretty busy, what with three girls to keep up with," my acquaintance would say, obviously wanting to hear more about Nancy.

"Yes, she's very involved with the girls," I'd reply, and then brace myself to deliver the bad news. Something like, "Unfortunately, she's not as involved as she'd like to be because she's battling breast cancer . . . "

It didn't matter what I said after that. When you choose to inform someone that your wife has a life-threatening illness, you're choosing to upset his equilibrium with a very unpleasant reality—which means you're opening yourself up to who knows what sort of reaction. And I got all kinds. Shock. Expressions of sympathy. Advice. Tears. Nervous chatter. Stunned silence. Apologies, as if the other person had done something wrong. Stories about their great-aunt Myrtle who had breast cancer and found a cure through an extract from apricot pits, and how Nancy just *had* to look into that because it's a miracle cure, even though there's a big conspiracy by the medical establishment to keep it off the market. I even had one person, who apparently could not

> People certainly want to be supportive. But they don't want to have your experience.

tolerate discomfort, come across with an effort at humor in a vain attempt to lighten things up.

I never asked for any of that. But that's what you get when your wife has cancer. And what's lonely about it is that while people genuinely want to know, in a way they *don't* want to know. People certainly want to be supportive. But they don't want to have your experience. What they want is to get through that unexpected moment that you've created for them, and then they want to go back to their routine and go home and kiss their spouse and hug their kids and watch TV and take their daughter to the mall to buy eye shadow to match the prom dress.

And I don't blame them in the least for that, because that's exactly what I wanted to do, too. But such a life was not given to me. Oh, sure, I kissed Nancy and I hugged my girls and I watched TV and the rest of it. But as I said earlier, my family and I lived at every moment, 24/7, sometimes consciously, sometimes unconsciously, but always, always with the uncertainty of how this "cancer thing" was going to turn out.

How do you communicate that to other people? Do you even want to? Do you really want to be the one who always brings the conversation to a screeching halt by talking about your sick wife? Do you even want to show up at things, knowing that people are going to ask because they care? You're so glad that they care; yet you're just weary of having to talk yet again about how Nancy is doing, and how the girls are doing, and how you're doing. At some point, you just want to go hide.

It's by such means that suffering manages to alienate us from others and make us feel very lonely.

JOIN THE CROWD

And yet, as I started to say earlier, while Nancy and I may have felt lonely, we found we were far from alone. For example, the first time Nancy went through chemo, she discovered a whole floor of people who, like her, were fighting for their lives. Each of them had a story.

There was the elderly lady who matter-of-factly announced that she just *had* to get better because, if not, she didn't know how her husband of forty-three years would manage. He had had a stroke, and she was his only caregiver.

There was the woman about five years younger than Nancy who came to chemo on her day off from work. Her husband had divorced her after her diagnosis (apparently, that's quite common, I learned). Now she had two small children to provide for, cancer or no cancer.

And then there was the retired guy who viewed chemo as nothing but a huge inconvenience to his golf game. Always decked out in checked trousers and sneakers, he constantly looked at his watch, fretting to get the IV out of his arm so he could go hit the links.

After Nancy went metastatic (meaning the cancer spread to other sites in her liver, lungs, and bones), she found an online support group of fellow "mets" people. Day after day they exchanged e-mails to trade thoughts, information, jokes, prayers, poems, news. It was a profoundly important community for Nancy to participate in.

The only downside was that longtime members would suddenly go silent. And sometimes it would be weeks or months before a survivor had the presence of mind (and the compassion) to send back word of that person's death. Sometimes the word never came. They were just . . . gone.

In short, we discovered lots of people sharing the House of Mourning with us. If I'm doing the math right, in the nearly four years since Nancy's death, 155,000 women have died of breast cancer in the United States. Whenever I hear about such a woman, or come across her obituary, I sigh, knowing there is a world of grief wrapped up in that one story.

Cancer is the number one cause of death for people Nancy's age (forty-seven), according to the Centers for Disease Control (CDC). The second is heart disease. And so, a few months after Nancy died, a neighbor up the street went jogging one morning, as he had for most of his forty-five years of life. With no warning, and for no apparent reason, he dropped dead on the sidewalk, his heart having failed. He left a widow and four small children. A company minus a valued employee. A community minus a solid citizen. More arrivals in the House of Mourning.

On an extraordinarily beautiful morning almost a year after Nancy's death, I boarded an American Airlines flight at Dallas's Love Field. We took off at dawn and landed at Chicago's O'Hare at 7:55. I don't think I've ever had a more peaceful, relaxing flight.

On the shuttle to pick up my rental car, a guy across the aisle looked at the person beside me and said matter-of-factly, "Did you hear what happened in New York? Someone crashed a plane into the World Trade Center."

All of us who heard him looked at him like he was a nut. But when I got to my car, the attendants were all buzzing about something happening in the Big Apple. Then I turned on the radio.

And so the towers fell, and the Pentagon burned, and the heroes forced the plane down in Pennsylvania. And I drove back to Dallas. And by the time I got there, the entire country seemed to have joined me in the House of Mourning.

And emotions that by then had become so familiar to me—anger, rage, grief, loss, loneliness, fear, confusion, depression, sadness, despondency, disappointment, frustration, touchiness, restlessness, tearfulness, resignation, stress, weariness, exhaustion—I found them wherever I turned as people were venting their feelings.

Few human activities present more pitfalls than trying to find the meaning in grief and loss.

Not always appropriately. Not always consciously. Not always willfully. For many, it seemed to be a whole new thing to experience life in such a way: to lose one's confidence, to no longer feel secure. To gradually become aware—and grieve—that maybe the party is over.

Very quickly, I started hearing and reading all sorts of analyses pretending to "come to terms" with what all these feelings meant. It's what people do when they first arrive at the House of Mourning. They grasp at quick, easy answers to deaden the pain. But later on, time and perspective reveal just how off point most of those early pronouncements turn out to be.

I can say that because, remember, I've spent ten years in the House of Mourning. And until now, I've refrained from making any pronouncements. You see, I have a strong aversion to embarrassing myself, and few human activities present more pitfalls than trying to find the meaning in grief and loss (consider Job's three friends). As my dad says, better to keep your mouth shut and let people wonder if you're a fool than to open it and remove all doubt.

However, sometimes life has a way of goading me into action. Something happens, and I *have* to say something. It's not like a choice. It's an assignment. A "burden," the Old Testament prophets called it. I was "burdened" into writing this book by the following incident.

While the leading cause of death for adults is cancer, the leading cause of death for younger ages is "unintentional injury," as the CDC categorizes it. In other words, accidents.

ON A SUNNY MORNING

In October 2003, I marked the third anniversary of Nancy's death. The next morning, a Wednesday, was another spectacularly gorgeous day, more like spring than fall (we don't really do fall in Dallas; we just open up the windows and let the air conditioning cool things down).

Anyway, it was the sort of day when all seemed right with the world. Sun shining. Leaves turning. Birds singing. Dogs barking. Parents hugging their kids good-bye. Neighbors waving on their way to work.

And a parade of schoolchildren walking, skipping, biking, and scootering their way to the elementary school just up the street.

A mother walks her two girls to the thoroughfare between

their block and the neighborhood of the school. Look one way. Look the other. No cars. Okay, it's safe. Into the intersection goes the four-year-old, then the mother, then the first-grader on her Razor Scooter.

Just then an SUV sitting at the intersection across the street pulls forward. Without warning, it turns left—right over the first-grader. Later, the driver would tell officers that he was blinded by the morning sun and never saw the little girl.

But three years and a day after I held my wife's hand as she slipped into eternity in a tragic and premature way, a mother just blocks from my house held her daughter's hand as she lay in the street and slipped into eternity in a tragic and premature way. And two more families, and classmates, and teachers, and neighbors joined us in the House of Mourning.

Where was God's lovingkindness for that precious little girl? That was the obvious question.

It was my responsibility on the following Sunday to teach the second of a two-part series to a class at my church. The first week I had spoken on God's lovingkindness from Psalm 136, which twenty-six times insists that God's lovingkindness is everlasting. And then that tragic "unintentional injury" occurred to a little girl in our community. I found myself silenced. And a bit embarrassed, to be honest. *Rebuked*, was how I felt. Rebuked by life and by "reality."

Where was God's lovingkindness for that precious little girl? That was the obvious question. Where was God's lovingkindness for that poor mother? Where was God's lovingkindness for the little sister who watched the whole tragedy unfold? Where was God's lovingkindness for the eighteen-year-old driver and his family? Where was God's lovingkindness for everyone else who loved those involved in the tragedy?

Psalm 136 says, "Give thanks to the LORD, for He is good, for His lovingkindness is everlasting."[2] Oh really? In what sense is it "everlasting"?

And what about that proverb I cited earlier? "It is better to go to a house of mourning than to go to a house of feasting." How so? In what sense is it "better"?

I had planned to teach on other things that Sunday. But the loss of that little girl just taunted me: "So, Bill, have you learned *anything* through your experience with Nancy's death that might be useful in a time like this?" The book that follows is what I ended up saying.

But before I say it, let me say this to the reader. As you may have guessed by now, I approach grief as a Christian, and I write from my perspective as a Christian. However, this book is not just for Christians. It's for anyone who knows grief, loss, pain, or suffering. Because the experience of those sorrows is universal.

I recognize that not every reader will share my beliefs. That's fine. My hope is that regardless of your faith, religion, or spirituality, you will benefit from my experience. Because should you ever find yourself in the House of Mourning, you'll discover a perfect cross section of the world. We've got people with all kinds of beliefs and disbeliefs about God here. And the interesting thing about mourning is that it more or less forces out what people really hold to and hold on to. What follows is what the burden of the last ten years has forced out of me.

TWO

Love
to the
Extreme

What do you think of when you think of God? I'll bet ninety out of a hundred people would say something like, "When I think of God, I think of love."

Of course, a lot of people who say that are not always happy with God. They may feel He's somehow cheating them out of a good thing, or not showing up as they face a bad thing. But the majority of people want to believe in God. And they want to believe He's a loving God.

One reason people believe God loves us is because the New Testament says "God is love."[1] That's pretty reassuring.

Except that when I'm standing in the checkout line at the supermarket, the glossy magazine says it's got "Ten Surefire Ways You Can Get Your Man to *Love* You More."

And when I turn on the radio on the way home, I can hit any channel and hear someone belting out passionate declarations of undying *love*. But wait! Didn't I just see that artist's name on the tabloid cover, exposed for having cheated on his/her mate in a steamy sex scandal?

And while I don't really watch so-called reality shows on TV, I'm at least aware of the premise of some of them: that someone is going to discover "true *love.*" Or if not, they at least get a million bucks. (Is that all "true *love*" is worth?)

HEBREW WORDS AND RUNAWAY BUNNIES

So what exactly does it mean that "God is love"? Well, long before the New Testament gave us those words, the Old Testament gave us a word to describe God's love. It's the Hebrew word *chesed.*

And what does *chesed* mean? Therein lies a problem. There is no single English word that quite captures its meaning. Various Bible translations render it in various ways: mercy, kindness, goodness, faithfulness, devotion, steadfast love, covenant love. In Psalm 136, where *chesed* appears twenty-six times, the New American Standard Version translates it "lovingkindness." What in the world does that mean?

When a word can't be translated directly, its meaning has to be arrived at indirectly by getting at the idea behind the word. The idea behind *chesed* is *commitment*—but the meaning goes beyond the contractual sense of the word. If you buy a house, you sign a contract that says you've paid money and now own the house. That's a business deal. *Chesed,* however, refers to the kind of commitment we call a "covenant," which means a pledge, an oath, a one-way door of commitment, a permanent decision to pursue a particular course of action or way of relating.

Let me give two illustrations of *chesed*. American Indian lore (at least, what I was exposed to growing up) has it that certain tribes practiced personal blood oaths between two braves. Each man would slice open his hand; then the two would join hands and mingle their blood, making them blood brothers. It was a sign that they were permanently committed to one another. They would fight on each other's behalf, and, if necessary, die on the other's behalf.[2]

That's a *covenant*. That's a one-way door of commitment. It is lifelong. There's no backing out. And it's fueled by love, by affection for the other person.

That kind of commitment may sound rather drastic. But there is a hint of the drastic in the idea of *chesed*. It goes beyond a cold calculation to passion. One *abandons* oneself to the commitment. In that sense, *chesed* is a bit irrational.

Which brings me to a second ilustration of *chesed*. As our three girls were growing up, Nancy and I read countless books to them. Among their favorites (and ours) was the classic picture book, *The Runaway Bunny*, by Margaret Wise Brown, illustrated by Clement Hurd. It's about a little bunny who keeps telling his mother he is going to run away and have adventures. Most of the adventures have a degree of danger and thrill and fantasy attached to them: swimming like a trout in a rushing stream, climbing a steep mountain, flying like a bird, sailing on an ocean.

In response to each imagined exploit, the mother bunny

answers with an idea of her own for how she will go after her little bunny and cause him to find his way back to her. In the end, nothing the bunny can suggest seems to be able to outwit his mother's relentless watchfulness. So at last he gives it up: "'Shucks,' said the bunny, 'I might just as well stay where I am and be your little bunny.' And so he did."[3]

Now the genius of Margaret Wise Brown is that in this very simple tale she gets to the essence of what it means to be a mother. The little bunny knows that he will *always* be the object of his mother's affection. She will never let him go. Her heart will always be for him and always be the home to which he returns. And it is the confidence of that bond that gives the little bunny freedom to venture out into a risky world—even if only in his imagination—and try himself against its challenges. Because no matter what happens, one thing is certain: his mother will never give him up. She will always show up for him.

I suggest that the mother bunny is a picture of *chesed*. For *chesed* is a matter of the heart—a heart abandoned in its devotion to another.

So now I've given you both a masculine and a feminine picture of *chesed* to illustrate that lovingkindness (let's use English now) means that God shows up for us when we need Him most. He has given His heart to us. He has committed His blood for us, and His life for us. His blood for our blood, His life for our life. He has abandoned Himself to that commitment.

Psalm 136 aims to make sure we never forget that fact. I encourage you to get a Bible and read that psalm now. You'll find that there is a rhythm to the verses. Each one celebrates

God for something He has done, then there's a chorus that tells what motivated God to do what He has done: "For His lovingkindness is everlasting."

Twenty-six times the psalm repeats that chorus—because that's the core truth. That's the theme. That's the underlying, never dying reality that we need to keep coming back to: God's lovingkindness is everlasting. God has pledged Himself —His own *Self*—permanently, always, without retreat, without reservation, without condemnation, with full power and authority to do so—God has pledged His life and His blood to faithfully, mercifully, and devotedly bring about His good on our behalf, in ways that vindicate us over evil. That's what God's lovingkindness is all about.

The psalm keeps repeating that truth in order to hammer home the fact that God's lovingkindness is more certain than anything else. It's the one fixed point in a world that seems chaotic and sometimes almost absurd.

AND IT WAS GOOD

We need to hear that core truth repeated over and over, because as true and certain as it is, the fact remains that we don't live in that truth. It doesn't hold our attention. What holds our attention most of the time is our experience in the real world. That's what the other lines in Psalm 136 are all about. The psalm praises God for His lovingkindness by giving examples of it in action in the real world.

For example, the psalm begins by saying that nature itself is an expression of God's lovingkindness. Have you ever thought of that? God's commitment to our good dates at least to the creation of the world, when He "made the heavens with skill," when He "spread out the earth above the waters," when He "made the great lights," the sun, the moon, and the stars. Talk about an everlasting commitment!

God's lovingkindness is built into the very fabric of the universe. It all exists for His pleasure. And just as Genesis says, the creation is "very good," just as the God who made it is very good.

One place that Nancy experienced that "very good-ness" was at the sea. Having grown up near Philadelphia, she and her family spent a lot of time at the Jersey shore in the summers. And all during the time we were married, she would periodically look up suddenly and announce, "I must go down to the sea!"[4] We would then make plans to get to the nearest coastline, whether Maine, Hawaii, Pawley's Island, or the Pacific Northwest.

Standing on the gray rocks at Ogunquit, feeling the percussive shock of many tons of water colliding thunderously against resolute granite, salt spray filling her lungs and raindrops pelting her face, Nancy was nothing if not in love with the world—a beautiful, alive world, with seagulls taunting just a few feet above, and remarkably tenacious creatures just below the waterline.

An occasional seal would break the surface with a gasp, as if to say, "C'mon in, the water's fine!" One time, a whale even came under the keel of our sailboat and lifted us several inches out of the water.

For Nancy, God's lovingkindness resided in the ocean. The experience of it filled her up with joy. How long has that ocean been crashing into Maine? That's how long God's lovingkindness has been crashing into the world.

So, too, the sun. I well remember the vacation during which Nancy made me get up in the middle of the night and drive twenty miles to the deserted parking lot of a national park. Grumbling and dubious, I hiked with her up a trail until we came to an overlook. Our surroundings gradually took form as the light intensified, like a Polaroid slowly developing.

And then, sure enough, right on time, a shaft of sunlight arced over the perfectly smooth horizon of the ocean and slammed into us on the top of Cadillac Mountain—tall enough and east enough to be the first land in the Northern Hemisphere to see the sun each morning.

> How long has that moon been dancing through the night? That's how long God's lovingkindness has been watching over a sleeping world.

How long has that magnificent sight been showing up? How long has that light been ripening the blueberries that we discovered up there, in bushes all around us? We ate until our fingers turned blue and our tongues turned purple. And later, back at the cottage, Nancy made muffins, and the butter melted into them, and the Earl Grey tea (her favorite) warmed us too.

> The LORD's lovingkindnesses indeed never cease,
> For His compassions never fail.
> They are new every morning;
> Great is Your faithfulness.[5]

Every morning. That's how often God's lovingkindness shows up. Every time the sun rips the horizon, spilling light over and into the world—pure energy that turns into heat and shadow, photosynthesis and color, aurora borealis and poetry. How long has dawn been showing that compassion? That's how long God's lovingkindness has been waking up the world.

But don't forget the moon and stars! These, the psalmist reminds us, God made "to rule by night."

Nancy and I used to read *Goodnight Moon,* another Margaret Wise Brown/Clement Hurd classic, to our babies before tucking them away for the night.

> In the great green room
> There was a telephone
> And a red balloon
> And a picture of—
> The cow jumping over the moon. . .
> Goodnight room
> Goodnight moon . . .[6]

Occasionally the moon would be positioned in such a way that it cast its light directly into the girls' room. As their eyelids drooped, did they know that that moon was just a lifeless rock in the sky, doing nothing more than bouncing light from the sun?

Or wait! Was it not put there for a purpose, as Queen of the Night, with subtle yet extraordinary power over the oceans, and over nocturnal creatures, and over the affections of lovers, and over the activity of emergency rooms, and over the visions of presidents, and over the fate of nations, and even over the menses of women? How long has that moon been dancing through the night? That's how long God's loving-kindness has been watching over a sleeping world.

Goodnight Moon!

Goodnight God! Moon-Creator. Human-Lover.

God's commitment to our good dates at least to the creation of the world.

AND YET . . .

Sometimes the world is quite beautiful. As a result, we feel quite wonderful. In those moments it's easy to think that, yes, of course there's a God. And isn't He a good God too? (Unless you're an atheist. As G. K. Chesterton observed, how awful it must be to have your heart well up in gratitude and have no one to thank for it.)

The world can be so beautiful. But sometimes the world can be quite terrible. Sometimes the ocean you were happily sailing on swallows your ship. Sometimes the morning sun you smiled to see blinds you from seeing the little girl on the scooter. Sometimes the man in the moon hides his face, giving the advantage to the man in the shadows who steps out with a knife.

It's not always a safe world. Sometimes the world is quite terrible. When it is, we can feel rather awful. Does that change who God is? Sadly, for many people it does. When life tastes like a fine wine, it's easy to praise the vintner. But if the wine should turn to vinegar and shock the palate with bitterness, guess who gets the blame?

For many people, thinking about God never rises above a fairly simple calculus that goes: God is love; but I don't feel so loved right now, so there must be something wrong with God.

I completely understand that way of thinking because there have been times in my life when I have thought exactly that. There were times when Nancy's cancer was such a complete and total bother—to her, to me, to the whole family, in every possible way—that I just threw up my hands in disgust. Disgusted with the situation. Disgusted with life. Disgusted with God. Philip Yancey writes of people who are disappointed with God. I was disgusted with Him at times. So was Nancy.

So, to return to my question, do those feelings change who God is? Well, they do unless God is absolute.

Now I know that in our culture, *absolute* conjures up extremists who feel a God-given right to lay down rules that are unbending, intolerant, prejudicial, self-righteous, and ultimately abusive for the rest of us. So some readers may object to my use of the term "absolute."

> Is God who He says He is, even if our feelings and perceptions about Him change according to the circumstances of our life?

But it's interesting that while "absolutes" are anathema when it comes to questions of religion and morality, no one seems to mind absolutes when it comes to engineering, accounting, or brain surgery. Ever driven your car onto a bridge that was constructed according to "relative" inches?

Ever invited a doctor to cut on you who says, "Yeah, I took anatomy in medical school—and here's what it means to *me*"?

My point is not to get into a philosophical discussion on the nature and meaning of absolutes. I'm just asking a question: Is God who He says He is, even if our feelings and perceptions about Him change according to the circumstances of our life?

Psalm 136 insists that nothing about us or our circumstances changes God in the least. God's commitment to our good extends to the most desperate of straits. The psalm recalls three stories of God's intervention on behalf of His desperate people. On three different occasions, three kings intended evil against the Israelites: the Egyptian pharaoh, Sihon the Amorite, and Og of Bashan (these three were very nasty characters—even their names sound like something out of *The Lord of the Rings*).

But listen to the language that Psalm 136 uses to describe how God dealt with these thugs: "smote," "brought Israel out," "strong hand," "outstretched arm," "divided," "overthrew," "slew," "rescued." Those are strong words. But they, too, express God's lovingkindness. Clearly, that lovingkindness is aggressive. God *fights* for His people.

If you go back and read the account of Israel's exodus from Egypt, you'll find a significant battle taking place between a determined God and a stubborn pharaoh. God deals out ten world-class plagues on the Egyptians—from the Nile turning to blood, to overrunning the country with frogs, to insects, to cattle dying, to boils, to hail, to locusts, to pitch darkness, and finally to the deaths of all the Egyptians' firstborn. Pretty brutal! But apparently that's what it takes to get Pharaoh to send the Israelites away.

Yet even after all of that Pharaoh reneges. And everything comes to a showdown at the Red Sea. The Israelites are in absolute panic. And just when it seems all is lost, God shows up. And when He shows up, He's not smiling. He's warring. First He parts the Red Sea to deliver His people; then He restores the water's flow to destroy their enemies.

Again: God *fights* for His people. That's His pledge. That's His commitment. His blood for our blood, His life for our life.

So if the world can turn terrible, God can turn terrible too. Terribly good. Terribly devoted. Terribly just in vindicating those to whom He has pledged Himself.

Interestingly, He fights for them despite their fear and complaining, because God's lovingkindness is not dependent on human beings. It is totally a function of His grace.

Now there's something to be thankful for—the fact that God's lovingkindness is not dependent on me and my complaining. God's lovingkindness is there in the oceans, and the sun, and the moon, and the stars . . . and, yes, in the violence that overthrows evil kings . . . and a thousand million billion other ways—*regardless of me*. Regardless of my feelings. Regardless of my disgust in a bad situation. Regardless, even, of my disgust with God.

God's lovingkindness depends on God. Even in the most desperate of our circumstances. And in truth, life as a whole turns out to be a pretty desperate situation. In the next chapter, I'll explain.

THREE

It's an Ugly Day in the Neighorhood

Do you remember Fred Rogers, the gentle, kind, courteous host of the PBS television show *Mister Rogers' Neighborhood*? When my girls were little, they loved to watch Mr. Rogers. I loved to watch them watching him. By the time Mr. Rogers was closing with his signature song, it truly was a beautiful day in the neighborhood.

Except for the day when the *Challenger* exploded, killing seven brilliant people and plunging a nation into grief.

And except for the day when Kristin woke up to find that something had gotten into the bunny hutch and done away with her bunny. How do you explain spatters of blood to a sobbing ten-year-old?

And except for the days when the chemo made Mommy too sick to get out of bed, even to retch. "Daddy, is Mommy going to be okay?"

I thank God for Fred Rogers. I thank God that Fred Rogers reminded us to look for the beauty in the neighborhood. But not even he could overcome the fact that on some days the neighborhood is ugly, not beautiful.

None of us wants to believe that. It's too depressing.

"Well, you're right about that," I can hear some readers saying. "Here I am in a bad place, looking for a bit of comfort, looking for something to cheer me up, and all you can do is talk about how bad the world is."

I certainly can identify with that. I can imagine that maybe you've picked up this book looking for comfort, and here I am talking about explosions and dead bunnies and chemo. So what's the point? That's what I want to know whenever I feel significant pain or have a burning question. I don't want someone beating around the bush. I want them to get to the point: "What is it that I need to know that will make things better for me?"

Most Americans are in denial about the reality of evil.

Well, the first thing you need to know might not feel very cheerful or comforting. But here it is: when you get to the House of Mourning, you should make yourself at home. You'll be here a while.

Does that feel cold for me to say? Does that summon a pang of grief? It's okay if it does. There's nothing to celebrate, really, when you enter the House of Mourning. People arrive with all kinds of "bad" feelings. Sadness. Anger. Depression. Rage. Many feel washed out. Listless. Used up.

Broken. A lot of us don't even want to think anymore. We're tired of having to—trying to—come up with answers.

Whatever your particular condition, I take no joy in welcoming you to the House of Mourning. None of us is glad to be here. But here we are.

I've been here ten years. That may seem like a long time. But time is not measured in years at the House of Mourning. It is measured in wisdom. Some who have just arrived astonish me with their insight into what is true, what matters, and what is valuable. Others have been here a lifetime, yet you'd never know it.

THE FACE OF EVIL

Time here is measured in wisdom. And the way toward wisdom begins by telling what you know, with what you can honestly say.[1] I know and can honestly say three things after ten years in the House of Mourning. The first is not particularly pleasant: I've learned that evil is real.

If you're thinking you already know that, don't be so sure. Odds are you don't. All indications are that most human beings, and certainly most Americans, are in denial about the reality of evil.

Consider the numbers. George Gallup has been polling Americans on their belief in God since 1944. Year in and year out, between 90 and 96 percent of us say that God is for real.[2] And overwhelmingly we believe in a personal God to whom we can relate, not just an idea or an impersonal Creator.

Moreover, almost everyone who believes in God believes in a *good* God. Ninety percent of us believe that God loves us, and 84 percent believe that God is actively involved in our lives. In fact, 85 percent of us believe we can count on God to take care of us in times of personal crisis.[3]

But now contrast that to belief in a force of evil—a devil or Satan. Only 68 percent of Americans believe that Satan is real.[4] How real? Certainly not as real as God. "Most American adults (59 percent) consider that Satan is simply a symbol or concept or principle of evil, not an actual personality," reports Barna Research. "Three in four Roman Catholics believe this; 55 percent of Protestants agree." Only "a minority of adults (34 percent) believe Satan to be a living being."[5]

There is really no surprise about these differing numbers. As I said in the last chapter, most people want to believe in God, and they want to believe He's a loving God. But who really *wants* to believe in evil? Who really wants to think that there are real, live forces at work in the universe aimed at the destruction of all that is noble? Set against all that is good? Enraged against any and every effort to carry out what is right? Supportive of every form of injustice, prejudice, hatred, betrayal, murder, deceit, error, cowardice, greed, perversion, selfishness, abnormality, sickness, tragedy, confusion—and any other conceivable type of wickedness?

None of us wants to contemplate that, do we? It's just too depressing. And yet, depressing or not, the world is what it is. We would be fools if we chose to deny or ignore reality.

Let me be clear: I'm a generally optimistic person who tries to hold on to a positive outlook on life. I don't go around seeing devils under every bush. I am not superstitious. I do not suffer from clinical depression. But I react quite strongly to the widely held perception that the world is just a fine place, and that people are basically good, and that if we'll just look on the bright side, things will always work out.

I'm not saying there's not good in the world. There is a *lot* of good in the world. But there is also a great deal of evil—certainly enough that the reality of evil seems to me undeniable.

Perhaps your parents did as mine used to do whenever my siblings and I complained about our food. "You should be thankful you even *have* food," my dad would say with that tone and that look parents get when they've had just about enough of their whiny brats. "Do you realize there are children in China who are starving to death? You get three meals a day and then some, and they'd be thankful just to have a single bite of what you've left on your plate."

Of course, I would think, *Then why can't we ship them my Brussels sprouts?* But as it turns out, my dad was right. During the very years that I was growing up in Dallas and griping about my dinners, the people of Communist China were being subjected to an economic restructuring that their leader, Mao Tse-tung, labeled the Great Leap Forward.

Operating on the principle that the "proletariat" class was the true and noble citizens of the state, Mao and his party were turning Chinese society upside down by such ludicrous practices as moving farmers to the cities and telling them they would now be doctors, and in turn relocating doctors (denounced as "capitalist roaders") to work the farms. Predictably, the results were disastrous. Some 30 million Chinese are estimated to have starved to death thanks to the Great Leap Forward. I can think of no better words to describe Mao's arrogant policy than idiocy, insanity, and just plain evil. Some might argue that he meant well but was misguided. But some of the worst evils in the world have been committed by those with idealistic zeal for making the world better.

I was born during the bloodiest century in the history of the world. By the time I came along, some-where around 35 million soldiers had already died in wars.

In the spring of 1975, the North Vietnamese army captured Saigon, and a war that had bitterly divided the United States came to its ignominious end. I was a junior in college making my summer plans on the day that the last helicopter lifted off from the roof of the U.S. embassy. I certainly didn't care to see Americans leaving in defeat. But I also thought, *I hope that part of the world can get a bit of peace now. They have suffered so much.*

Little did I know that only two weeks earlier, an army called the Khmer Rouge had entered Phnom Penh, the capital of Cambodia, Vietnam's neighbor to the west. The army's arrival brought a five-year civil war to an end. But it didn't bring peace. On the same day that the Khmer marched into the city, they began evacuating its citizens to the countryside in a zealous campaign to recover some idealized notion of Cambodia as a traditional agrarian society of peasants (referred to as the "old people"). Business owners, executives, professionals, educators, artists, and any other Cambodians with education or skills were considered enemies of the "old people," and the new leaders began systematically exterminating them.

The slaughter continued for four years until Vietnam finally attacked and pushed out the Khmer Rouge. What the Vietnamese found was a land literally pockmarked by thousands of mass graves. In all, somewhere between 1.7 million and 2 million Cambodians are believed to have died at the hands of their own countrymen.

When I began reading reports about the Cambodian killing fields in the early 1980s, I remember doubting them at first. It seemed incomprehensible that genocide of that magnitude could have occurred during the very time when I was meeting Nancy and falling in love and picking out an engagement ring and getting married and going on our honeymoon and settling into our apartment on Sparhawk Lane. *Millions* of deaths? No way, I thought. That's the sort of thing that we did away with when we got rid of Hitler and Stalin. Surely civilization wouldn't permit millions of people to be slaughtered like that nowadays.

But I was flattering myself to think that I somehow lived in a better world than my forebears. In truth, I was born during the bloodiest century in the history of the world. By the time I came along, somewhere around 35 million soldiers had already died in wars. Two and a half million more would lose their lives before the millennium ended.

Those are sobering numbers. But the staggering number is the estimated 187 million individual men, women, and children who were killed in the twentieth century through genocide. Genocide requires more than an army. It requires an entire society to organize itself around the elimination of a particular group. Which means that everyday people—people just like you and me—in some way end up contributing to the systematic killing of their neighbors.

That's what happened in Cambodia. And to the Armenians (1.5 million deaths). And to the Tibetans (1.6 million deaths). And to both Croats and Serbs in Bosnia (200,000 deaths). And to Jews in Germany (6 million deaths). And to the Nuer and Dinka peoples of Sudan (2 million deaths). And to the Ibos in Nigeria (1 million deaths). And to the Mayans in Guatemala (200,000 deaths). And to the Kurds in Iraq (190,000 deaths). And to the Kurds in Iran (60,000 deaths). And to the Kurds in Turkey (10,000 deaths). And to the Kurds in Syria (21,000 deaths). And to Hindus in Pakistan (61,000 deaths). And to "class enemies" in the U.S.S.R. (15 million deaths). And to "enemies of the people" in the People's Republic of China (10 million deaths).

I could go on and on. You get the point. In fact, that *is* the point—that I could go on and on. Millions upon millions of people cut down by their fellow man. And the most chilling thing is that the people doing the killing almost always believed they were making the world better by eliminating their victims.

So then, what's the connection between the bungled economics of the Great Leap Forward or the massive genocides of the twentieth century, and my wife's death in October of 2000? Simply this: in both cases we're talking about death. But whereas the deaths of people in rice paddies or labor camps are known to me only as sobering statistics and disturbing headlines, Nancy was Nancy. Nancy was a face, and a voice, and a person, and a presence. Nancy was my wife.

Nancy was the mother of our three children. Nancy knew my name. Nancy knew the best of me. Nancy knew the worst of me. Nancy knew my heart.

TOO CRUEL, TOO FINAL

And so when it was Nancy's death that I had to stand by and witness, this whole matter of evil got personal. Evil was no longer an idea; evil became real. And by that experience of Nancy's death, every other death that had ever taken place in this world somehow became more real to me—as if I could relate to the pain of each one. And a dark conviction began to settle in my mind: the awareness that something exists in this universe that really does want us dead, by whatever means it takes.

None of us wants to believe that. It's just too depressing.

Indeed, maybe that desire not to know helps to account for the considerable lengths to which we Americans go to avoid the subject of death. The word "death" itself is hard for many people to come right out and say. I became hypersensitive to that as Nancy approached the end of her life and finally died. I've noticed it with every death I've been around since. People have a hard time saying the words "death" or "died." Those words seem too cold, cruel, and insensitive. And too final.

So instead, we use euphemisms like "her passing," or "when he passed away," or "his untimely end." Likewise, obituaries speak gently: the person "departed this earthly life," "fell asleep," "entered into eternal rest," "passed on to glory," "lost her battle," "was called home," . . . and on and on.

I remember when my older sister Barb died. Our family was met at the funeral home by a rotund fellow in a black suit with a white shirt whose starched collar strained against his beefy red neck. I admit that I was not in a particularly cheerful mood to begin with. But as we walked to the conference room to discus the arrangements, I kept thinking, *Can we lose the cologne?*

He sat at the end of the conference table and folded his hands. It was time for him to go to work. So, as if someone had flipped a switch, he cocked his head, blinked a couple times, smiled in a faux-angelic sort of way, and said, "Well, folks, I'm sorry we have to meet under circumstances like this."

> No one, to my knowledge, was able to say to her, straight out, "Nancy, you're dying."

And I thought, *Under what other circumstances would I want to meet the likes of you?*

I know, I know. I'm being mean-spirited. The man was just doing his job. He's probably a decent fellow in real life. But that's the point. When it comes to death, we suddenly have a hard time sticking with real life.

Nancy was ill for seven years. During all that time, no one—no professional, no counselor, no friend, no relative— no one, to my knowledge, was able to say to her, straight out, "Nancy, you're dying."

She knew she was. The rest of us knew she was. But somehow neither she nor we wanted to have that conversation. It was not an issue of denial, but avoidance. Death is just an

an important truth that the House of Mourning offers: that evil is real.

I thought I had known that. I certainly grew up knowing that bad things happen in the world. But they happened to other people, not to me or mine.

So yes, I knew *about* evil. But then I came to know evil. I looked him in the eye. And by that encounter I discovered that the world turns out to be just as the Bible says it is: fallen and under a curse.

Not a comforting thought, is it? It was certainly not a thought that anyone was keen to remind me of when Nancy was in the throes of her suffering. To do so would have seemed utterly thoughtless and insensitive, right?

But day after day, I could feel the truth that no one wanted to voice: "Something is wrong here. This isn't the way it's supposed to be. This isn't what God intended. This dark place that Nancy and I and our girls are in is in fact *not* something we should be particularly happy about, because this dark place was not really meant to be, even though it is."

I would encourage the reader to reflect on your own experience. Do you feel that same way sometimes? If so, there's a word for that feeling, as we shall see.

FOUR

Life: Why Bother?

My sister's favorite store in the whole world is Crate & Barrel. Bev absolutely loves that store. And so it was that she found her way back to the Crate & Barrel that used to be at Dallas's NorthPark Mall while Christmas shopping several years ago.

NorthPark was in an utter frenzy of people in a holiday mood. The pandemonium was exciting, but overwhelming. So, seeking respite from the crush of the crowd and its festive din, Bev took a turn into the Crate & Barrel just off the center court of the mall. At last, she had entered an oasis of order, civility, taste, and refinement. Strategically placed halogen lighting made the whole place sparkle with vivid colors, highlighting no end of accoutrements for the kitchen and dining area. All was in perfect array. All was set up to appeal. All was crying out to the customer as she ogled the wares: "Take me home! Take me home!"

At the center of this dazzling picture was a massive pyramid of stemware. Gorgeous wine goblets stacked on a glass table in ascending rows of luminescent crystal, perhaps eight feet high. The display itself was a work of art, and no one who entered the store could miss it.

Bev certainly did not. As she came upon the table, she observed the unique shape of the glasses and, like any curious shopper, decided to examine the product more closely. A lone wineglass had been set there for such a purpose, so she picked it up.

At that point, time suddenly stood still. The scene went into slow motion. The wine glass was in Bev's hand. The hand was raising it to the light. The light was just beginning to dance off the glass and sparkle in her eye. Her eye was just beginning to examine the design. And just then, out of the corner of that eye, she saw a glimmer from the display. The slightest quivering, like the tremor of a wee earthquake. She felt an impulse to steady the table. But as if in a dream—or a nightmare—her arm would not move, could not move. It would have been pointless if it had. For in one massive plunge, the entire display of stemware collapsed to the hardwood floor, which, like the underside of a grand piano, amplified beyond all imagining an agonizing, ear-splitting crash.

Then there was silence.

Heads turned. Store personnel looked up. The security guard whipped around. Babies quit their crying and blinked. All eyes were fixed on the ruin of glass at the center of the store. And on Bev standing next to it, holding a solitary goblet in her hand—the only goblet still intact.

Wide-eyed, speechless, utterly incredulous, Bev turned in shock to a lady standing next to her. At which point the lady stiffened and announced, "Well, I didn't do it!" and marched off.

By now people were streaming in from the mall to see what had happened. Bev looked around in vain for someone to rescue her from this terribly embarrassing predicament. Finally the store manager arrived, and Bev began pleading her case. "I don't know what happened! It just collapsed! I just picked up a glass! Honestly, I was just . . ."

"It's okay, ma'am," the manager interrupted her with a calming voice. "I'm just glad you're not hurt."

"No, I'm not hurt. I just don't know how I'm going to pay for this!"

"Don't worry, ma'am, we carry insurance to cover things like this."

And so, after Bev assured the manager that she really was all right, and he assured her that everything really was okay, she finally was able to do the thing she had wanted to do since the instant the display had collapsed, and that was leave the store.

Which was not as easy as it sounds. A pretty good-sized crowd had gathered. People were staring and pointing at her. As they parted to let her through, she could hear whispers among them: "That's her," or "She's the one." Suddenly the seasonal chaos of the mall seemed oddly inviting, and Bev quickly and gladly blended into the crowd so as to vanish into anonymity. Not surprisingly, she never did return to that particular Crate & Barrel.

"NOW WHAT DO I DO?"

I tell this story about my sister—with her permission, I hasten to add—because it provides a great analogy for the human condition. You see, when someone we love is taken from us prematurely, when the city is outraged by a senseless killing, when terrorists break into a school and slaughter innocents in the name of heaven, when our minds are reeling with the ugly legacies of megadeath that I mentioned in the last chapter, when the world seems anything but safe and life is turning out to be a nasty business, we *do* get the feeling that we are looking at something terribly wrong. Something is not as it should be. Confronted with the agonies of this world, we feel as if someone has picked up a goblet and the entire display has crashed to the floor.

I felt that way after Nancy died. In 1993 we were fifteen years into building our family, and the pyramid was pretty far along. Nancy and I certainly had challenges to surmount in our marriage, but the good news is we were working on those. Meanwhile, we had these three incredible girls who were just in love with life and about as eager to embrace the best that the world has to offer as three little girls could be. So by November 1993, there was already a lot of shine and sparkle to the five-sided tower we were putting up. Anyone could see that this was going to be a pretty impressive structure.

Then the phone call came. "Mrs. Hendricks, this is Dr. Knox's office. Dr. Knox needs to see you right away. Can you come in this afternoon?" Instantly Nancy knew by the tone of the nurse and by the urgency to schedule the appointment that she was facing her worst nightmare: breast cancer.

I held her as she collapsed into sobs, raw fear emanating from her throat. And the words, over and over again, "I'm going to die! I'm going to die! Oh, honey, I'm going to die!" It was pointless to point out that we had not even heard the diagnosis. Nancy knew in her gut before she even met with Dr. Knox that this "thing" was ultimately going to be the death of her. Turns out she was right.

After she died, I did have that feeling of, "What happened? Things were going along so well. Nancy was just living her life. So was I. We were trying to build a family, just minding our own business. Yet here I am with a lot of broken glass all over the floor. Now what do I do?"

"IS THAT IT?"

There's a word for what I was experiencing. It's the same word for what many have experienced the morning they woke up to a new and very unpleasant reality that they'd never expected and certainly never asked for. Whatever that morning and whenever it dawned, they woke up and thought, *What's happened? I didn't expect this. I don't want this. I don't want to have to deal with this. This isn't what I want for my life.* And eventually, hemmed in by the claustrophobic fact that "this" is indeed what they are stuck with, the quandary arose: *Now what am I going to do?*

If you've ever been at that point, you were experiencing the Hebrew word *hebel*. *Hebel* is the experience of having one's hopes and expectations dashed to pieces. It's having the rug pulled out from under you. It's picking up the goblet— the goblet of a spouse, or a baby, or a career, or a house, or a trust fund, or a business scheme, or a political cause, or a philosophical position about life—and there are no end of goblets that humans pick up and rely on as sources of hope and stability—anyway, you pick up the goblet, and next thing you know there's a crash, and suddenly you're standing in bewilderment, blinking at the shards of your expectations scattered here and there across the floor. You're disappointed. You're frustrated. And you have a sick feeling of doubt about life itself, a sense of disillusionment: *Is that it? Is that what life turns out to be? I had hoped for so much more.*

> But I wasn't looking to get cheered up. Cheer could change my mood, but it couldn't change my outlook. For that I needed insight.

That's the experience of *hebel*. The essence of the word has to do with something fleeting, transitory, empty. It's like a vapor or a puff of smoke. Something is right there where you can see it—and then it's not there. It has vanished away.

There's also a sense of disappointment in *hebel,* and a sense of frustration. Have you ever labored at your computer for a while on some involved task, like a writing assignment or a spreadsheet or a layout? And then, just about the time you've gotten to the point where you're satisfied with your work, your computer crashes, or you inadvertently delete the file, or you lose your computer altogether. How do you feel when you realize that all your effort has gone for naught? That feeling is a tiny taste of *hebel*. It's the feeling of futility.

In the scheme of things, a lost computer file is usually

fairly inconsequential. But things get more serious when something you are basing your life on vanishes. Something you believe in, something that holds out promise, something you are counting on. Just when you most need that thing that you most care about—it's gone! It's no longer there. And when that happens, you suddenly feel like you're standing in midair, gaping in bewilderment and with nothing to support you. Worse than feeling shocked, you feel betrayed. As if life has let you down.

That's the experience of *hebel*. Futility.

When I was in the middle of Nancy's ordeal, I turned frequently to a book in the Old Testament that is entirely devoted to the experience of futility. That may strike you as an odd thing to do, since I guess most people in my situation would be looking for something to cheer them up. But I wasn't looking to get cheered up. Cheer could change my mood, but it couldn't change my outlook. For that I needed insight. I found it in the enigmatic book of Ecclesiastes.

Ecclesiastes is all about life "under the sun," as the writer puts it.[1] That is, life down here on planet Earth. Life on this side of heaven. The writer examines area after area of human experience—from nature, to food and drink, to commerce, to government, to law, to power, to money, to wisdom, to folly, to religious devotion, to love, to birth, to youth, to old age, to succession and inheritance, to death. He examines each area and says, "Here is what I have seen," and then he pronounces a conclusion.

His overall conclusion is this: "All is *hebel*."[2] All is futility. All is fleeting, transitory, empty, vanishing. Everything "under the sun," everything down here on earth, everything we humans experience on this side of heaven is tainted in some way by futility. *Everything*.

My intent here is not to make you feel depressed by discussing life's emptiness. But I'm a strong believer in facing reality as it actually is. I'd rather have the truth straight out and deal with it than avoid it because I'm afraid I might have a negative emotion. I can deal with my emotions. I can't deal with unreality.

And when Nancy and I and our girls were plunging into the abyss, I wanted to know reality. I wanted to know whether what I was facing had any connection to something meaningful. Or were my family and I just the butt of a cosmic joke? In sifting through all the things I had been told about the nature of the world—from parents, from friends, from books, from teachers, from ministers, from poets, from filmmakers, from comedians, from musicians, from the lifetime of voices collected in my head—I kept finding my way back to Ecclesiastes.

And Ecclesiastes presented me with reality. Not a pretty reality but certainly one that matched my experience. The more I examined the book, the more the pieces added up: I was living in a fallen world. Not an absurd world. A *fallen* world—a world where, time and again, evil shows up, leaving futility in its wake. A world, to be sure, where a great deal of beauty and goodness remain. But the beauties and the goods are like so many shards of shattered glass, reflecting light, yes, but with only a hint of their intended glory. And the more my eyes look at those beauties and those goods against the backdrop of *hebel,* the more I perceive the dark truth of a distant promise: "Your eyes will be opened, and you will be like Him, knowing good and evil." Oh, yes, I know good and evil now. But did I ever really *want* to know evil? Was I ever really *meant* to?

"THE PLANTS ARE COMING UP!"

Now, for the good.

In a world of futility, the writer of Ecclesiastes tells us, there are some valuable gifts that God gives us in the midst of this precarious life. They are quite simple gifts, really: food, family, work, laughter. Ecclesiastes tells us over and over that if we are given those sorts of things, we should take joy in them. They are gifts from God's hands in a world marked by *hebel.* It is also a gift if we can enjoy them.[3]

I have been given remarkable gifts in the midst of my own life "under the sun." Nancy herself was a gift. As I've already alluded to, Nancy was a planner. Once she got an idea in her mind for something that needed to happen, she could put together all the steps needed to get from here to there. And then she'd work those steps with relentless determination.

When she and I moved to Dallas from Boston in 1982, she decided that she had to have a vegetable garden. I tried to explain the challenges of gardening in Texas. But she dismissed all that. I'm sure she was thinking, *What does he know?*

First she went to Weldon Vaughan, our landlord, and got his permission to dig up the yard. A gardener himself, he was only too obliging, and he gave her counsel on how she needed to prepare the "black gumbo" soil that is prevalent in Dallas.

Then she went to several nurseries and talked with the

people there about what sorts of vegetables would grow best. In the end, she settled on beans, tomatoes, and squash.

I'm ashamed to admit that I stayed inside in the air-conditioning while Nancy labored in the Texas sun, turning over the soil and picking out the grass. Every once in a while I glanced out the window. She was working hard. But she was happy.

The next day she put the seeds and plants in and watered them down. And when she was done, she looked up and smiled. The plan was under way!

Every morning for the next few weeks, Nancy was out the back door at first light with a cup of tea. She'd stand by the garden and review its progress. Occasionally she'd stoop over or squat down, straining to see if anything was coming up.

One morning she rushed back inside, all excited. "Bill! Come look!" I trudged outside with her, not exactly feeling like Mr. Enthusiasm. She took me over to the garden and pointed. "See!"

I stooped down. A tiny shoot lay on top of the soil. Another one like it sat close by.

"They're coming up!" Nancy cried.

I continued to study the situation for a moment. "I don't know, Nance. You sure it's not just weeds?"

"Of course it's not weeds! They're coming up! The plants are coming up!" She was giddy with excitement.

Well, of course, she was right. But so was I. Within a couple days, we—or rather she—had a nice little patch of vegetables sprouting up, along with various kinds of weeds. Nancy took great delight in pulling those out.

Then one day, disaster struck the garden. The bean plants began to wither.

"I don't know what's going on!" Nancy declared in frustration. She watered them more. Then she worried that she'd overwatered. She aerated the soil. She covered the plants with shade. In the end, they lay down on the dirt, as if gasping for air.

Nancy's mood turned glum. But she was too angry to abandon the project. So she kept at it. And finally she discovered the root of the trouble (no pun intended). "Fire ants!" she shouted as she came through the back door. "Fire ants are eating my beans!" Was she mad!

Sure enough, in the middle of the beans was a fire ant mound volcanoing up, with a handful of ants scouting the terrain.

"How dare they?" she exclaimed, her fists clenched.

I came to discover later that our backyard was a fire ant sanctuary. I never could find any nests on the ground, though. But we always wondered why the gorgeous pecan tree that Weldon had planted in the middle of the yard never yielded any pecans. Until I climbed up into the tree one day and discovered that the fire ants had made the crotch of the tree their home—and the pecans their main supply of food. Thieves! And they had already robbed Nancy of her beans! Thankfully, Weldon showed us how to wipe them out.

Nancy still had the tomatoes and the squash. But long after tomatoes should have been popping up on the vines, all she had to show for her labors were a couple of puny, sickly looking balls. Her disappointment was palpable.

"I'll bet you got aphids," Weldon told her one day when

she was complaining about the situation. We looked carefully at the underside of the leaves. Sure enough, we found whitish, hairy mites glued to a sticky film.

"What a godforsaken place this is!" Nancy declared of Texas. "You can't grow *anything* here!"

She sprayed the plants, and the aphids eventually went away. But all in all, the tomato crop was a bust.

"Well, at least I've still got the squash!" she said resolutely, as the summer heat descended in earnest.

She regarded the squash as her ace in the hole. Squash, she told me, is the easiest thing in the world to grow. And it yields a lot of fruit. She reminded me of our friend Elaine Dibbs in Marblehead, Massachusetts, who grew so much squash one year that by the end of the season she was giving away shopping bags full of it.

Unfortunately for squash, Texas is not New England.

We were standing by the garden one evening, talking and occasionally bending over to pull out a grass shoot that had strayed into the plot. All of a sudden, Nancy let out a cry. "Hey!" She was batting at one of the plants. "Get off there!" She flicked a bug off the leaf and shook her head in disgust.

"Look, there's another one," I pointed out. She batted at that one too.

"Wow, look here!" I showed her three more on another plant.

"Honey, they're eating my plants!" She had tears in her eyes. "What are they?" she asked, looking at me like I was to blame. I shrugged.

As usual, Weldon Vaughan supplied the answer. "Squash bugs."

It was now a fight for survival! Nancy armed herself with some spray and began to fend off the squash bugs. But despite her efforts, the insects always managed to regroup and launch another offensive.

"It's a godforsaken place, I tell you!"

At that point in time, I had never heard the word *hebel.* Didn't matter. Nancy and I were getting an introductory course in the meaning of the concept.

Well, every evening after dinner, Nancy was out at the garden, picking off squash bugs one by one. And sure enough, a few small squash began to grow. Never were any squash watched over more or better than that handful of squash. It was as if Nancy was on a mission from God to ensure that those squash made it to our table.

And one night they did. As I sat down to dinner, Nancy turned from the stove with a look of utter vindication. She set a bowl on the table. It was steaming with squash. A little butter. A little seasoning. I think she had put a little Parmesan cheese on it too. I don't know what all she had done to prepare it. All I know is that I had the good sense to say, "Wow, this looks great!" She was smiling with pride.

And you know what? That squash *was* great. It may have been the best I've ever tasted. But who cares whether it was? What *mattered* was that Nancy had eked out a few decent squash from all of her labors. That was terribly satisfying to her. And the squash tasted great. And we enjoyed talking and laughing about what it had taken to grow those squash. And I was proud of her. And I was married to her, committed to her. And we were happy. And we had created a moment in our life together. A memory.

And so when Ecclesiastes says, "Here is what I have seen to be good and fitting: to eat, to drink and enjoy oneself in all one's labor in which he toils under the sun during the few years of his life which God has given him; for this is his reward," I have found that to be utterly true.[4]

Even in a fallen world, God grants us simple gifts, simple rewards.

And when Ecclesiastes tells me to "enjoy life with the woman whom you love all the days of your fleeting life which [God] has given to you under the sun; for this is your reward in life and in your toil in which you have labored under the sun," I have found that to be utterly true.[5]

I have found that life "under the sun" is indeed marked by *hebel*. Futility. Not absurdity. Life is not pointless. It has meaning. But life is marred by an inevitable futility—whether it's squash bugs in the garden, a retirement plan gone kaput, or cancer in a breast.

Yet there's grace, even in a fallen world. Even in a fallen world, God grants us simple gifts, simple rewards. Like a bowl of fresh squash. Like the smile of a spouse. Like the laughter of a good joke. Like a garden—bugs and all.

Is this beginning to sound like a "stop and smell the roses" message? It's not. It's a little more serious than that.

You see, Nancy loved to garden. But a few years later, she was too ill to work a garden. When that happened, she came upon the gift of being able to buy her squash at the Farmer's Market. And then the day came when she was too ill to go to the Farmer's Market. And when that happened, she came upon the gift of having friends who would buy squash for her. And then the day came when she could not taste the squash, because the chemo took away her sense of taste. And when that happened, she came upon the gift of watching her family enjoy the squash, even if she could not.

I'm all for stopping to smell the roses. But Ecclesiastes reminds us that it's a gift to be able to smell at all. And sometimes there aren't any roses—at least, none that you can see. Ironically, that's exactly the point at which many people who, like me, describe themselves as Christians have a particularly hard time sticking with reality.

FIVE

The
Glacier

Imagine the Bible in geographical terms. Some parts feel like broad, open plains. Others are picturesque harbors. Some are pretty deep oceans. Some are more like valleys.

And then there are the mountain ranges. Many of the Psalms feel that way. And in the New Testament, you have Romans. Indeed, for Christians the book of Romans may well be the Himalayas of the Bible. The book towers majestically with theological truth—challenging truth, not easily scaled. But for those who make the effort and avoid the pitfalls, the view from the top is spectacular.

If you'll indulge me to extend this metaphor, I would say that Romans 8 is the Mount Everest of all of Scripture. It is one magnificent, triumphant chapter, dominated by two massive peaks. On the front side stands the immovable declaration that "therefore there is now no condemnation for those who are in Christ Jesus."[1]

On the back side rises an even more impressive summit, built by a succession of ledges that stack on top of each other higher and higher until they are lost in the clouds of God's glory: "For I am convinced that neither death, nor life, nor angels, nor principalities, nor things present, nor things to come, nor powers, nor height, nor depth, nor any other created thing, will be able to separate us from the love of God, which is in Christ Jesus our Lord."[2]

Wow! What an incredible statement. Sort of takes your breath away. It's crystal clear. It's as solid as iron. It's the culmination of everything presented in Romans 1–8. Indeed, if I can switch analogies, that passage is the "Hallelujah Chorus" of Romans. You almost feel like standing up as you read it.

DON'T FORGET!

In the last ten years, I have been told repeatedly to not forget those last two verses of Romans 8. Countless people, concerned for me as well as for Nancy and my family, have brought me/us back to that climactic view.

They have done so, I believe, out of sincere concern. They are worried that perhaps in the midst of my troubles I have forgotten or will forget the truth about God's steadfast love. No one has ever told me that explicitly (although one or two have come pretty close). But it seems clear they feel that way by how quickly they have brought me back to Romans 8.

I have since discovered that's also the experience of many others in the House of Mourning. For example, a sister is raped and killed. A husband dies in a freak car crash. A cousin finally succumbs to a lifelong battle with cystic fibrosis. A spouse of sixty-eight years expires in the night, leaving an eighty-six-year-old widow feeling all alone in the world.

However it comes, the moment comes. And very quickly thereafter come voices. Sometimes they are gentle voices. Sometimes they are quite forceful and insistent. Some of them, I daresay, are downright cruel. But however they come, the voices come with one basic message: "Don't forget God loves you!" "Don't forget God will comfort you!" "Don't forget that God is with you!" "I know you must be hurting, but don't forget that nothing can separate you from God's love!"

> I have known people for whom the loss of a loved one marked the point at which they began turning away from God.

I'm of a mixed mind about the value of such counsel. I hesitate to even say that, because for one thing I'm liable to offend all of the people who sent me and my girls cards and e-mails and gifts and money and other expressions of kindness in the aftermath of Nancy's death. For me to say that I question the value of such support probably sounds ungrateful and downright insulting.

So let me reassure anyone who is thinking that: I thank God for the outpouring of love, compassion, support, and assistance that we received both before and after Nancy died. I still have every card, letter, and e-mail that came to me during those days, and I still read them from time to time. They were and are gifts from God's hand—gifts like the ones described in the previous chapter, gifts of grace in the midst of a futile, tragic situation in a futile, fallen world.

So how can I be of a mixed mind about reminders of God's love and goodness? Well, on the one hand, it's absolutely true that God's love continues on, despite whatever loss, suffering, pain, injustice, tragedy, heartache, or trial we find ourselves in. That's the truth of those last two verses in Romans 8, and it's a reassuring truth, I can say from personal experience. Thank God for those verses!

I also think there's value in hearing that truth repeatedly, because grief has a way of tempting a person to doubt God, to question His love, to dwell on one's troubles and losses and negative feelings, instead of on God. In fact, I have known people for whom the loss of a loved one marked the turning point in their life—the point at which they began turning away from God, embittered and doubtful of His goodness.

LEWIS'S BROKEN HEART

Indeed, we should pay attention to the experience of C. S. Lewis, arguably the greatest apologist for Christianity in the twentieth century. Many of his writings, including such classics as *Mere Christianity, The Problem of Pain,* and *The Chronicles of Narnia,* remain best sellers to this day.

In 1956, Lewis married Joy Davidman, sixteen years his junior, in a civil ceremony. At the time, he claimed that the marriage was a mere formality, that he was only helping a single-parent mother with cancer avert deportation. But the marriage blossomed into a deeply loving relationship. As he put it to a friend, "I never expected to have, in my sixties, the happiness that passed me by in my twenties." (Lewis was quite aware that his friends joked about the double meaning his marriage lent to the title of one of his books, *Surprised by Joy.*)

But Lewis's happiness was short-lived. Joy died of cancer in 1960. And according to Chad Walsh, a longtime friend, her death "plunged Lewis into the very depths of despair. His religion, which had seemed so sturdily based, began to crumble. A meaningless or malevolent universe opened up at his feet."[3]

That's a remarkable statement: "plunged into the very depths of despair." Only a few years earlier, this same man had boldly asserted, "Faith, in the sense in which I am . . . using the word, is the art of holding onto things your reason has once accepted, in spite of your changing moods" (or emotions). How does it strike you to know that the man who wrote that saw his brilliantly reasoned religion begin to fail him when his wife died?[4] What does this say about the universe, that at any moment it is capable of dashing the hopes and dreams of a sixty-eight-year-old saint to smithereens?

> "The conclusion I dread is not, 'So there's no God after all,' but, 'So this is what God's really like. Deceive yourself no longer.'"
> —C. S. Lewis

We should take heed to what happened when Lewis came face-to-face with the dark eye of that fallen universe. His faith took a tremendous blow from which he never fully recovered. To put it bluntly, C. S. Lewis, the great Christian apologist, was effectively silenced. He never wrote another significant work, and he died only three years after his wife. I think a case could be made that he died of a broken heart.

Why do I say that? Because in the months after Joy's death, Lewis kept a journal of his experience. It makes for interesting reading, because instead of the masterful arguments and crisp, witty prose of his earlier works, the journal is written in choppy spasms of thought. And what does it mean that Lewis eventually published those writings under an assumed name, rather than his own? Clearly, the death of Joy shattered his confidence, and nearly shattered his faith.

After his death, *A Grief Observed* was republished under Lewis's real name. Early on in it, he pinpoints the challenge to a person's faith when they suffer severe loss: "Not that I am (I think) in much danger of ceasing to believe in God. The real danger is of coming to believe such dreadful things about Him. The conclusion I dread is not, 'So there's no God after all,' but, 'So this is what God's really like. Deceive yourself no longer.'"[5]

There you have the human condition. As I've said repeatedly, we *want* to believe in a God. And most of us do believe in Him. But we struggle with whether He's a good God. Because this is such a fallen world, where such terrible things happen. And when they happen to *you*—when evil gets personal—all bets are off on how you're going to react the next time someone tells you, "Don't forget God loves you!" "Don't forget that nothing can separate you from His love!"

If you had told C. S. Lewis that sort of thing after his wife died, you know what he would have said? "Where is God? This is one of the most disquieting symptoms. When you are happy, so happy that you have no sense of needing Him, so happy that you are tempted to feel His claims upon you as an interruption, if you remember yourself and turn to

And so we were back to just the four of us—me, Brittany, Kristin, and Amy.

I remember how I felt after they were off to school that Monday morning. I came home, and the house was quiet. I sat down in the overstuffed blue chair—the one I'd always regarded as "Nancy's chair"—and just sat for a while.

In silence.

And the silence felt wonderful. And it felt awful. Wonderful and awful, all at the same time.

It felt wonderful, because as unbelievably helpful and supportive as all the people had been, it was the first moment when I had really had the benefit of solitude and silence since . . . well, since I could remember. Years, probably. It felt wonderful, because at last I had a respite from the noise. At last, I could just be still.

And oh, how I needed to just be still!

Yet in the stillness, there was silence. And the silence was awful. Not because it highlighted Nancy's absence. I felt that later. On that day, the silence was about death. I was silenced in the face of death. I had nothing to say. I, lover of words, craver of meaning, orchestrator of perspective. I, who had said so much to so many in the days and the weeks before. I finally had nothing to say.

There was nothing anyone could say. It seemed to me that the only meaningful response to what had happened was to just be silent. To just be still, and let the full weight and impact of Nancy's death come washing over me—however it might do so.

I think it was in that moment, on that morning, that I finally realized I had come into the House of Mourning. And what I needed to hear at that point was silence. And that need continued for some time. Eventually I needed to hear other things. But for that moment, and for a while thereafter, I just needed silence.

I would advise anyone who mourns, for whatever reason, to actively pursue the discipline of silence. That will probably be hard to do. The easy thing will be to stay busy. Indeed, well-meaning friends may think they are doing you a favor by finding ways to occupy your time. "We don't want you to get down in the dumps," they'll tell you. "We just thought we'd come cheer you up."

PAYING ATTENTION

Even if your friends leave you alone (which can also happen, because they don't know what to do with the awkwardness), you can slip into patterns that *avoid* solitude and silence. Such as watching TV or DVDs, or going to movies, or shopping, or spending extra time with your kids. Or working. Or catching up on all those chores you left undone when you were in crisis mode. Or even reading. Just because you are by yourself doesn't mean you are silent. Just because you are doing something quiet doesn't mean you are silent.

Silence means that you clear your attention. That you put away as many distractions as possible. That you give your insides a chance to be still, a chance to pay attention to *you*—whatever happens to be there.

For many people, that can be kind of scary. But you need to do it.

I needed the silence to be in touch with the pain. You

see, there's an odd thing about grief and pain. Most of us avoid pain at all costs. And if we're in pain, we just want relief from it. We want out of the pain as quickly as possible. But the odd thing about grief and pain is that the way out of the pain is through the pain. People who get "stuck" in grief are people who refuse to let themselves experience the pain of the grief.

And that's why I'm uneasy about encouraging people to "look beyond" their feelings of loss and hurt by trying to refocus their attention on the truth that "God loves you." That's moving too quickly. It's depriving them of the opportunity to gain wisdom from their sorrow.

But I can see why quite a number of people who know someone experiencing loss or suffering impulsively tell them, "Don't forget that God loves you!" Oftentimes the ones offering that advice are themselves unwilling to accept pain. They just don't want to hear about it. When they come across someone who is hurting, they start hurting along with that person—which is about the most human thing there is, by the way. It's called empathy. But quite a number of people won't put themselves in circumstances where they can empathize with those in real pain. They are unwilling to enter into another person's suffering.

> But how can He be with us in our pain if we refuse to be in the pain?

Why? Because pain and suffering are a direct assault on the very truth that nothing can separate us from God's love. That's what the Romans passage says. Yet here is someone utterly undone by circumstances that seem beyond bearing.

So how do you put that together? How do you reconcile what Christians hold to be absolute, eternal truth with un-deniable human experience that appears to contradict that truth? The answer, for too many of us, is to ignore the pain. To deny the emotion, as if it didn't matter.

Believe me, it matters!

It matters enough that God gave us an entire book of the Bible (Ecclesiastes) in which He says, in effect, "I completely understand your experience of living in a fallen world. It feels empty and frustrating and fleeting and futile, doesn't it?"

God does not want us to deny pain. I am coming very soon to the "good news" of this book, which is that God is prepared to be with us in our pain. But how can He be with us in our pain if we refuse to be in the pain?

God gives us permission to feel the pain—right in the middle of Romans 8. For sure, we must never lose sight of those grand and glorious mountains on either end of that passage. The one declares that nothing can condemn us if we are in Christ. The other insists that nothing can separate us from the love of Christ.

But nestled between those magnificent peaks is a steep valley. And in that valley is a glacier, very deep, very heavy, and very dark. Indeed, like most substantial glaciers, the ice is so dense and solid that it has turned dark blue. And, like most substantial glaciers, it has gouged a significant scar on the terrain.

That glacier is named Futility: "For the creation was sub-jected to futility, not willingly, but because of Him who sub-jected it, in hope that the creation itself also will be set free from its slavery to corruption into the freedom of the glory of the children of God. For we know that the whole creation groans and suffers the pains of childbirth together until now. And not only this, but also we ourselves, having the first fruits of the Spirit, even we ourselves groan within ourselves, waiting eagerly for our adoption as sons, the redemption of our body."[8]

That's an extremely important passage for those of us in the House of Mourning. It reaffirms the truth of Ecclesiastes, that we live in a fallen world—a world subjected by its Creator to futility.[9] And guess what? When we experience that futility, we *groan.*

Which means that the pain we feel is legitimate, and to be expected. Indeed, if someone doesn't groan when accosted by the fallenness of this world, we need to be concerned about their health and the condition of their humanity.

Romans 8 gives us permission to groan. Do we give ourselves that permission? Do we allow ourselves to feel the pain? To cry the tears. To beat the pillow—or the wall—with bitterness? Or anger? Or grief? Or loss? Or emptiness? Or exhaustion? Or whatever? Is that okay? Romans 8 says it is. Do we?

Irrational? You bet. Seemingly out of control? Perhaps. But during the last ten years, I have learned that it is occasionally necessary to go a little bit crazy so as not to go completely insane. Romans 8 reassures me that God doesn't seem to mind if I go a little bit crazy when tossed about like a rag doll by the futility of this fallen world.

SIX

"Where Are You?"

"Once there was a little bunny who wanted to run away. So he said to his mother, 'I am running away.'

"'If you run away,' said his mother, 'I will run after you. For you are my little bunny.'"[1]

So begins the whimsical tale of *The Runaway Bunny,* which I mentioned earlier in the book. It's the story of a little bunny who keeps teasing his mother that he is going to run away and have adventures. Each time he tells her that, she replies that he will not get far, because she will come after him.

I said that the mother bunny's vigilant devotion to her little bunny goes to the essence of what motherhood is all about. And, in fact, I believe that that sort of motherly devotion, relentless in its commitment, is a great picture of what God's lovingkindness is all about. "If you run away, I will run after you," says God. "For you are Mine."

The desire for that kind of devotion is quite primitive on our part. As near as I can tell, it begins from the womb and never goes away. Whether young or old, we all want to know that someone cares about us. We also want to know that Someone cares about us.

Within two or three minutes of the moment that Nancy died, Kristin and Amy, who had been in a lounge area outside her hospital room, pushed the door open and started into the room (Brittany was already in the room). "Girls," I said, looking up, "Mommy has just died. Just now." The two of them stopped in their tracks, taking in what I was telling them. I nodded. "She died just a minute ago."

They eyed the bed, where Mommy lay. I could read the uncertainty on their faces as to what this meant, and what they should do. "Do you want to come in and be with her?" I asked them. Kristin nodded and quietly moved forward. Eight-year-old Amy, on the other hand, stayed put.

"Do you want to come in, Ames, or just stay outside?" Her response to this second prompt was to shake her head and take a slight step backward. I thought I detected fear in her eyes. Seeing that, there was no question in my mind what I needed to do—*wanted* to do. Letting go of Nancy's hand, I stood up and walked to the door and picked up Amy in my arms and walked out into the hallway. I just stood there holding my little girl for I don't know how long, the two of us crying together.

Then, without warning and without the slightest hesitation, Amy asked me point-blank, "Daddy, are you going to get married again?"

Let me tell you, that was the last question I was expecting to be asked on that particular day. And from my youngest daughter, no less! A thousand thoughts flashed through my mind, and ten thousand questions. I mean, what do you say in answer to a question like that?

But suddenly an answer was given me, heaven-sent I feel sure. "Ames, I don't know if I'll remarry," I began, "but I know one thing. Daddy's here with you and Kristin and Brittany. Even though Mommy's gone, Daddy's here, and I'm not going anywhere. Daddy will take care of you."

Amy looked at me—looked me right in the eyes. She nodded and then hugged me tightly. I carried her down to the end of the corridor, and we sat down on the floor by the narrow, floor-to-ceiling window. I began humming a lullaby, the tune to the Christmas hymn, "Once in Royal David's City." I used to hum that melody to all three of the girls whenever I tucked them into bed. I had always found it to be a calming influence at the end of the day. So it seemed a fitting way to bring some calm to Amy—and to me —in the immediate aftermath of Mommy's death. I hummed it through a couple of times. When I finished, we just sat

> What hurts the most about that loneliness is that most of us instinctively feel that the person who ought to be right there with us in our ordeal is God.

for a while, saying nothing, watching the sun, which had been hidden behind gloomy, drizzly clouds all day long, make one last grand appearance on its way to kissing the horizon goodnight.

WHERE IS THE MOTHER BUNNY?

The Runaway Bunny is about what happens if the little bunny should run away. But what happens if it's the mother bunny who is taken away? In that case, the little bunny is left with a question: Who is going to take care of me now? That was really the point of Amy's query. Now that Mommy is gone, who is going to take care of me? Who is going to come after me? Who is going to be my mother bunny? Or am I on my own?

That question is not limited to eight-year-olds. In truth, it's the question all of us ask when the bad stuff happens. It's a form of the question, where is God?

At the beginning of the book, I mentioned the loneliness that Nancy and I felt in the midst of our particular troubles. That's a fairly universal experience for people facing tragedy and suffering and pain. Even if they have a superb network of support around them, as we were fortunate enough to have, at some level they still have the sense that they are going through their trials alone.

But what hurts the most about that loneliness is that most of us instinctively feel that the person who ought to be right there with us in our ordeal is God. Because God is the ultimate Mother Bunny. God is the One who has said His lovingkindness is everlasting. God is the One who has said He will run after us. So then, when the suffering comes, when we fall into the fallenness of this fallen world, we ask the question, where is He? As Philip Yancey has put it in his perfectly titled and outstanding book, *Where Is God When It Hurts?* Where is our Mother Bunny? Where are the Everlast-

flash flood, even as the firefighter reached out to grab her? Where was God for the two little children in my community whose mother lost her mind one night and stabbed them to death in the upstairs bathroom? For that matter, where was God for that poor, deranged woman whose hold on reality exploded into psychotic madness? And for the horrified father who found all three of them dead?

"Where was God?"

"Where was God?"

"Where was God?"

No matter how great your faith and no matter how positive your outlook on the world, you can't watch the enormous pain and suffering and tragedy that take place every day and not be struck by the thought that something is terribly, horribly wrong. There's supposed to be a God, and a loving God at that. Yet even the people who stake their lives on that belief find themselves at a loss sometimes to have any sense of His presence. It's like He's . . . gone!

And that's really the ultimate tragedy about the human condition. When the bad stuff happens and evil comes our way and intrudes itself such that we cannot deny it, escape it, reason our way out of it, buy our way out of it, pretend our way out of it, drink our way out of it; when the pain is present and real and hurts like hell—the ultimate tragedy is that we feel cut off from God. Abandoned. Totally on our own. And we end up wondering, whispering, pleading, crying out: "Where is God?"

GOD'S QUESTION TO US

There is, of course, an answer to that question. And I would like to get into that answer by pointing out something that I don't think I've ever seen acknowledged by people who talk about grief and loss and pain. It turns out that God is asking the same question of us! God is calling out, "Where are you?"

Did you know that? God asks the exact same question we ask. But not with anger and blame, the way we do. When we ask, where is God? we're usually feeling as if we've been wronged, as if the Someone who should have been taking care of us has let us down. But God asks the question differently.

Go back to *The Runaway Bunny*. Imagine that the little bunny follows through on his threat and actually runs away. What will the mother bunny do? Why, go looking for her little bunny, just as she said she would. And how do you suppose she will call out to him, especially if he's managed to get himself in trouble? She will go all over, crying out, "Where are you? Where are you?" She will keep searching and calling out until she finds him and takes him home. Well, that's the motherly devotion with which God calls out to us as human beings. In effect, He goes all over, crying out, "Where are you? Where are you?"

Some readers will doubt that. Especially if they've felt abandoned by God. But consider this: when God came looking for Adam and Eve after they had run away (in every sense of the term), that's how He called out to them: "Where are you?"[3]

Does that not strike you as odd? That God would *come after* two people who had done the very thing He expressly told them not to do? Yes, He was displeased. Infinitely displeased. Yet instead of running away from them, He ran after them. That only makes sense if God's heart was completely devoted to His human creatures. If His heart was for them— just as the mother bunny's heart was for her little bunny, just as my heart is for my daughters—then it makes perfect sense that God's primary concern when Adam and Eve got in trouble would be to come after them and find them, no matter what they had done.

No matter what they had done. Do you get that? It's very important that you do. God's lovingkindness is not conditioned on the behaviors, motives, or actions—good or bad— of humans. I stress that because some readers are living with a tremendous guilt that their sufferings are the result of some terrible thing they have done. They believe that they *deserve* whatever heartache has come their way. They've dealt with the question of God's whereabouts this way: "God has abandoned me because He's punishing me."

> God's heart is still *for* you, regardless of whatever terrible thing you have done.

If you're thinking that, I don't think you understand God.

Many years ago, a friend of mine was told by his wife that she had been having an affair. After stunning him with that awful news, she rushed to her lover—who happened to be someone I also knew. In short order, the two left town for a weekend together.

I was shocked. My friend was devastated. He spent that entire day holed up at home, sitting in the dark, wondering what had happened, what was going on, and what he was going to do about it. Then, late that night, he called me. When I answered the phone, he asked one simple question: "Bill, do you know where my wife is?" I'll never forget the anguish in that man's voice. He was utterly broken and desolate.

I believe that when God called out to Adam and Eve, His voice was similarly anguished. "Where are you?" He cried out to them. It was not a question that He asked from His mind or His wisdom or His understanding. God knew exactly where Adam and Eve were. God knows everything. Nor was it a question designed to shame them or even to call them to account. They already felt ashamed, and He would call them to account later. No, when God called out to those two cowering souls, He was calling out to them *from His heart.* The question reveals God's heart.

And so I say to the person who feels as if your suffering is God's justifiable punishment for something you have done: God is not punishing you; God is calling out to you. You may have done a terrible thing. My friend's wife did a terrible thing. Yet even after she slapped him in the face with blatant, brazen adultery, his heart was still *for* her when he called me up and asked, "Do you know where my wife is?"

Similarly, God's heart is still *for* you, regardless of whatever terrible thing you have done. Yes, He knows you have caused trouble. He also knows you are in trouble. And to you He calls out, "Where are you?" Whenever you are ready, you can come out of hiding and respond to His call. Sure, you'll need to admit some wrongdoing. Sure, you'll need His forgiveness. Sure, you'll need to make apologies and amends to people you have hurt and wronged. But never doubt God's lovingkindness. Never doubt that His heart is calling out to you.

WHAT ABOUT THE INNOCENTS?

Okay. But . . .

I can hear someone pushing back at me. I can almost see someone squirming in her seat as she reads this chapter. I can almost read her mind, and it's thinking something like this: *Bill, what you say is very true. God certainly loves sinners. I won't disagree with that. That's all well and good. But you're not making an apples-to-apples comparison here. Adam and Eve did something patently wrong and ended up estranged from God. But what about people who did absolutely nothing to deserve what happened to them—people like Nancy and her loved ones, or the little girl on the scooter and her loved ones, or the people in the Twin Towers and their loved ones, or the people in the Holocaust and their loved ones. People who didn't do anything wrong! Yet in their hour of trial, they felt abandoned by God. Okay, so maybe God called out to Adam and Eve. Why doesn't He call out to innocent people who are calling out to Him?*

Who says He is not?

I concede that innocent people die. I will not concede that God turns a blind eye toward them. The question, where was God? assumes that He does. But who is in a position to say that? I certainly am not. Are you?

Look, there is an awful lot about the awful stuff that happens in this world that remains a mystery to me. And a deeply troubling mystery at that. One mystery is that on one side of suffering there are human beings with the question, where is God? And on the other side is God calling out, "Where are you?" Whatever else one might say about that situation, it's obvious that something is terribly, horribly wrong. Surely that is not what God intended. Yet there it is anyway.

As a human, I can easily end up blaming God for that mess. Not like He caused it. But why doesn't He just fix it? If He's so powerful, why can't He just speak a word, like He did when He created the world, and make everything right? He's supposed to be the God who can do miracles. Why couldn't He just pass His hand over Nancy and take her cancer away? He is said to have done away with Pharaoh's army at the Red Sea. Why couldn't He just have done away with the Nazis, or killed all their first-born? If God is so powerful, why doesn't He put a stop to all this evil?

> How God goes about fixing the world? He's more like a roustabout than a magician.

I think you can imagine that I've pondered that question quite a bit over the past ten years. I don't know that I have any more insight or answers than anyone else. But I will say this: the question misunderstands God. It also underestimates evil.

A lot of us, when we say that God is "powerful," are thinking that He is like a magician or sorcerer who can wave a wand and do magic. All He has to do is snap His fingers, and He can alter reality. Well, if God were a magician, He obviously would have changed everything to perfection long ago. The fact that He hasn't says He isn't a magician and things don't work that way. That's not to say that God is not working. It just means that God's way of fixing the world is apparently not through a magic trick. Because it takes more than magic to do away with evil.

SAVING JESSICA

Do you remember the story of Jessica McClure? In October 1987, eighteen-month-old Jessica fell into an abandoned well behind her house in Midland, Texas. The pipe was only eight inches wide. After falling twenty-two feet down the shaft, the toddler became wedged with both arms and one leg up alongside of her head. Cold, scared, alone in the dark, Jessica kept crying out for her mother—who eventually found her. But what could the mother possibly do? What could anyone do? The situation looked hopeless.

TV crews began arriving to capture the drama. Soon the whole country was standing vigil to see how the incident would turn out. Various schemes for rescuing the little girl were put forth—none of them satisfactory. Time was running out. Finally a crew of oil-patch roustabouts came up with what everyone agreed was a long-shot strategy. First they had to dig down through rocky soil until they were just below where Jessica was stuck. Then they had to dig sideways until they hit the pipe. Then they had to cut a hole in the pipe large enough to extract the baby girl. What made these efforts especially precarious was the danger of dislodging Jessica—which would have sent her plummeting to certain death—or harming her through the noise and vibration of the machinery.

The rescuers worked nonstop for fifty-eight hours. But their relentless persistence paid off. Late on the third night, an EMT was sent down into the hole. When he came back up, he was holding baby Jessica, and a sea of onlookers cheered and wept with joy. "She's out! She's alive!"

Now I maintain that the rescue of Jessica McClure is a great picture of how God goes about fixing the world. He's more like a roustabout than a magician. He doesn't try to wish evil away. Because evil defies wishes. Evil is cruel. Evil delights in dashing hopes. Evil is stone hard and gritty and weighty and deep and dark and deadly. Evil is real. So God gets right into that reality, however messy and tough and precarious it may be, and He goes to work—taking care not to harm the very people He has come to help.

Unfortunately, a lot of the time the people He comes to help can't see His help. I know, because I've been there. For seven years, Nancy and I fought a ferocious battle against the evil of her cancer. By the end, I was utterly spent. And I felt utterly alone, as if abandoned by God. In truth, I often thought about baby Jessica at that time, because that's exactly how I felt—like I was stuck in a pipe with my leg up beside my head, wedged tight in a suffocating space, losing strength by the day, cold, scared, and alone in the dark.

When you're in a place like that, it's impossible to see that Someone is digging a shaft to come get you. In fact, it's impossible to see anything in the dark. All you can do is wait in the silence, with whatever thoughts and feelings you have—and a lot of those thoughts and feelings are not very pleasant. Needless to say, it doesn't take very long to start wondering, "Does anybody know I'm here? Does anybody care? Does God know I'm here? Does God care?"

In the end, your options boil down to two. You can give up hope and decide that God isn't going to show up. Or you can do what Jessica McClure did. Early in the rescue, the paramedics lowered a microphone to monitor the trapped girl's breathing. But how can you hear the breath of an eigh-teen-month-old? You can't unless she's making noise. And so Jessica's mother stayed by the pipe and kept calling down to her daughter. I can imagine she sent down all kinds of reas-suring messages. "It's okay, baby, help is on the way!" "Don't be scared, honey, Mommy's right here!" And to keep Jessica calm—and to make sure she was still all right—Jessica's mother got her little girl to sing.

So there was the scene: a frantic mother, no end of fire and rescue crews and paramedics, four hundred volunteers, news media, lights, heavy equipment, the whole world watching—all of that focused on an eight-inch pipe coming out of the ground in West Texas. And from that pipe, if you were quiet enough to listen, came the soft little sound of a baby girl's voice as she sang while she waited in the dark: "Winnie the Pooh! Winnie the Pooh!"

How could any child possibly be able to sing in a horri-ble situation like that? Because if your mommy's voice keeps coming down the pipe, telling you it's going to be okay, you trust that, because it is, after all, Mommy. You can trust Mommy. Mommy won't leave you in a fix. Mommy will come after you. Even if there's strange noises that make it so you can't hear Mommy's voice, you still know that she hasn't forgotten you. Because Mommy will *never* forget you. She can't forget you. Because Mommy is Mommy. Mommy's the devoted one. Mommy's the committed one. Mommy's the one with relentless lovingkindness.[4]

"'If you run away,' said his mother, 'I will run after you. For you are my little bunny.'"

In the rest of the book, I will tell you some ways that the Mother Bunny has run after me.

SEVEN

How Sunday School Saved My Life

I can't remember a time when I didn't go to church. I know that isn't true for everyone, but I grew up in a family where church mattered—a lot. Why, I've been going to church since nine months before I was born.

And the church I grew up in was the kind that made a big deal of Sunday school for the kids. It was very formal and intentional. The chairs were lined up in straight rows, lecture-style. The teachers stood at the front. It was "raise your hand, otherwise no talking, please." There was a set schedule of activities. And they gave us tokens to mark our achievements, like ribbons or badges or prizes, almost like grades in regular school.

I don't know whether that approach to Sunday school could work today, or whether it's even the most effective way to teach children. I do know that thanks to that system,

I learned a vast amount of basic Bible knowledge and basic Christian doctrine.

And so I owe a great deal of gratitude to Jeannette Prinz, who taught us the creation story. And to Win Bush, who played the piano and taught us hymns. And to Margie Seay and Bea Campbell and Jeanne Hendricks and Nita Lincoln, who must have taught us several hundred Bible stories using flannel graph (a sort of dinosaur media technology—maybe the ultimate precursor to PowerPoint). And to Jean Joseph, who put up with us in what was called Junior Choir. And to Merwin Seay, who motivated us to memorize many key passages of Scripture. And to so many others that I don't have space to mention.

For the most part, these people were not trained educators. They just believed that kids ought to learn what the Bible says. And so they volunteered for the job. I was one of the beneficiaries of their service.

In a little while I will tell you just how beneficial their service turned out to be when I was dealing with Nancy's cancer. But first let me point out that there can actually be a downside to growing up in that sort of background.

THE KNOW-IT-ALL

When you grow up in a church and Sunday after Sunday for eighteen or so years you hear the stories, doctrines, creeds, history, and traditions of the church repeated again and again and again, they eventually become locked in your brain. Indeed, they become written on your heart. They become part of you.

They especially become part of you if, as in my case, you actually come to believe the truth of those things, and your faith is more than just a ritual or a set of concepts that you give mental assent to but is a vital, experiential *trust* that you place in God on the basis of reasonable propositions.

In short, if you grow up in a church like the one in which I grew up, and you pay attention, eventually you come to know all the answers to most all of the questions they ask there.

And to its credit, our church asked some really good questions. Some really hard questions too. Like, if God is so good, why is there evil? And if God is so powerful, why doesn't He put a stop to it? Why do innocent people suffer? Where did evil come from? Is God really going to punish people who've never heard about Him? If God knew we were going to sin before He made us, why did He make us in the first place?

Please understand, my church didn't throw these questions at us in the second grade. But by the time I was in high school, we were routinely exposed to numerous questions like these. And by the time I graduated and went off to college, I had a decent grounding in Christian apologetics.

That gave me a lot of confidence. It also created a problem, what you might call an unintended consequence of "growing up Christian."

You see, I knew all the answers. I just didn't know what they meant. I didn't know their significance, because I lacked experience. I didn't know what I didn't know.

That's a real problem. Indeed, I worry about it with my own daughters. How do you help them embrace what is true

when they don't have a clue as to why that truth is important? It's not that they are necessarily opposed to the truth.
But how deeply can they believe in something that has yet to
matter one way or another in their life? They don't know
what they don't know.

And so, lacking experience, what happened for me happens for many who "grow up Christian." Our faith becomes
like the Pledge of Allegiance. Millions of us grew up reciting
the pledge almost every day at the beginning of school. As a
result, we memorized it cold. Indeed, if we had to, we could
come out of a dead sleep at three in the morning and recite
the pledge word perfect. So there's no question that we knew
the pledge. The question is, did we know anything about allegiance? Probably not, because at that age we had never had
our allegiance tested.

In a similar way, I knew as early as three years of age that
we live in a fallen world. I just didn't know how fallen the
world turns out to be. For instance, they taught me that people are sinners, which means they do bad things. That made
all the sense in the world to me, even at three years of age.
Especially *me* at three years of age!

What I didn't know was that the slender, freckle-faced,
blonde-haired girl who lived across the alley and was one of
my best friends throughout elementary school would grow
up to be abducted, along with her fiancé, taken down to the
Trinity River bottoms, tied up, sexually assaulted, forced to
watch her fiancé die, then be shot in the head herself, left for
dead, and then, after all of that, have to go through the whole
ordeal all over again when the matter came to trial, only to be
shocked when her abductor was handed a relatively light sen-

tence, so that she now lives with the fear that when he eventually gets out of prison he could come after her again.

I didn't know what I didn't know.

FROM KNOWING TO EXPERIENCING

They taught me that marriage is a holy covenant, which made sense to me. So at age twenty-three, I stood in front of God, the state, family, and friends at Christ Church in Hamilton, Massachusetts, and, when asked whether I would "love Nancy, comfort her, honor and keep her, *in sickness and in health*," I declared firmly, "I will!" And I meant it.

That commitment allowed me to be with Nancy every day thereafter and admire, among other things, her long, straight, dark brown hair, hair that she had not cut since high school, so that it draped down her back almost to her waist.

What I didn't know was that one day she would go to a clinic and have an IV inserted in her arm, and that a set of chemicals would be infused into her system that attack fast-growing cells—like cancer cells, but also like the cells that generate hair—and that within a few days those hair cells would become brittle, so that the hair would begin to break off at the roots and fall out and

> We're inviting people into unhealth if we tell them, "Don't pay attention to your experience."

tear out in clumps in Nancy's fingers, and make her scalp all itchy and irritable, so much so that after enduring it for a day or two, she asked me to get a pair of scissors and an electric shaver and cut off her hair—her beautiful, magnificent hair, her glory—which I did in the bathroom while she sobbed and I felt sick to my stomach doing something that felt cruel and kind all at the same time.

I didn't know what I didn't know.

The great problem of "growing up Christian" is that you grow up knowing answers with your mind, but you have yet to live them out through your experience.

And there is a whole tradition of Christians who say that that shouldn't matter, because our experience doesn't determine what is true. And I believe that: our experience doesn't *determine* what is true. But our experience certainly determines our appreciation of what is true.

And that is why I said earlier that I think it is a grave mistake to tell someone to ignore their feelings and their subjective experience, and just "trust God." I will come very shortly to how it is that we *can* trust God. But we're inviting people into unhealth if we tell them, "Don't pay attention to your experience." If we say that, we're telling them to stop dealing with reality.

Reality, as I have tried to point out, can be very messy. It defies easy answers. And sometimes reality isn't about answers at all. Sometimes it's about nothing loftier than coping and just trying to get through the day.

How do you explain any of this to a three-year-old? Or even an eighteen-year-old? Even an eighteen-year-old like me, who went to church Sunday mornings, Sunday nights, Wednesday nights, and countless other nights and days every week for eighteen years, and paid attention, and actually read his Bible every day the way you're supposed to, and even studied it and memorized it?

Make no mistake, that background has proved invaluable. But let's face it, no matter how much a kid may have taken in growing up, one simple fact remains: An eighteen-year-old doesn't know what he doesn't know. I grew up and went into the world knowing all the right things, for all the right reasons, with all the right intentions. But, lacking experience, I didn't know what I didn't know.

It was like being trained to fight as a knight, yet never having met a dragon. They told me there would be dragons. And they told me as best they could what a dragon is like, and how you fight one. Then I actually met one. Nothing quite prepares you to meet a real dragon. Maybe that's why so many of the people I've talked with who have met dragons in their own lives have ended up disillusioned. "Everything they told me is wrong," they've said with some bitterness.

WHEN I MET THE DRAGON

But here's where the tide turns. When I met the dragon, I came to exactly the opposite conclusion. When I encountered Nancy's cancer, and experienced all of its impact on her, on me, on my kids, and on just about everything else in my world, I came to see that *what the Bible says about the world is utterly true.* Only it turns out to be *more* true than I had realized—and true in ways that I hadn't realized.

That stunned me. That absolutely stunned me. "Wow! It's all true," I found myself saying. "It's just like it said. There really is evil. It really is real. There really is a force or power or something at work that could be so despicable and so malicious and so evil that it would hunt down a young mother the way a lion chases down a gazelle from behind, and snatches her in its claws, and wrestles her to the ground, and toys with her while she writhes on the ground, and finally takes her neck in its powerful jaws and bites down hard until the breath goes out of her. Meanwhile, three fawns stand by, watching their mother being taken from them. Is that evil, or what?"

It was just like it said. Just like what said? Just like who said? It was just like *God* had said. In the book I had been reading since before I could read.

And this is where my upbringing saved my life. You see, I didn't come to my conclusion—that what the Bible says about the world is true—overnight. Or even over a few days and nights. It happened over months and years. For months and years I, too, wrestled with the lion. There were times when I thought that the lion would squeeze the life out of me, just as it did Nancy. Sometimes I still think that.

> Sunday school loaded me up with some ammunition that came in mighty handy when the chips were down.

But over those years that the lion scratched and clawed and snarled at me and drew blood and breathed its putrid stench of death right in my face, an amazing thing happened: little snatches of Bible verses came percolating up into my consciousness. At the oddest moments, out of nowhere, for no particular reason, I would suddenly remember a phrase or a thought from the Bible.

Nothing prompted that. No one told me to do that. It just began happening. It was like a voice suddenly speaking inside me. Just matter-of-factly recalling a text—texts that I had known since time out of mind. Very simple little phrases, usually.

I'd be in the middle of a mess, or spiraling down into a morass of depression or anger or whatever emotion, and quite unexpectedly I would have this *awareness* of a Bible text. I say "awareness" because it wasn't like I heard voices (thankfully!). But it also wasn't like just remembering something. It was like . . . well, the best way I can describe it is that it was like a presence in my mind, the *presence* of some truth that I had taken in years and years ago. Only now that truth seemed more real or more *true* than I'd ever realized.

But it doesn't matter how I experienced those truths. That's irrelevant. The point is that the phrases or thoughts that came to me gave insight or perspective on whatever I was facing at the moment. Indeed, sometimes they helped me just to see *what* I was facing at the moment.

That saved my life. It certainly saved my sanity. And that's why I give quite a bit of credit to all those people who taught Sunday school way back in my childhood. I don't know what happened back there, but whatever it was, it loaded me up with some ammunition that came in mighty handy when the chips were down.

For that reason I want to pause right here and say a word to anyone reading this book who teaches Sunday school or works with young people. Having "grown up in the system," if you will, I've observed that Sunday school tends to get no respect. I mean, isn't it true that most churches have to beg for volunteers to teach Sunday school? And haven't you heard someone diminish someting's significance by joking, "What do think this is, a Sunday school picnic?"

I detest that attitutde! Given my background, you can see why. I believe that Sunday schools have a real serious job to do: They exist to prepare boys and girls for battle. The battle for good, and against evil.

Oh, I'll be the first to admit that Sunday school is a rather odd way to prepare someone for battle. I mean, think about it: if you are the Devil, and it is your intention to devour people's souls, you probably wouldn't be too alarmed by a Sunday school class, would you?

It's a bit like Goliath setting his eyes on David. The kid came armed with a slingshot. Imagine that! They sent a kid with a slingshot up against a nine-foot giant, armored and armed to the teeth. No wonder Goliath cursed with rage that the Israelites would insult him so![1]

I can imagine that the enemy of our souls laughs and curses just as much when he sees a Sunday school class. He says, "Ha! Is that the best you can do? What a joke! Here I am, getting ready to take this little boy when he grows up and put him and his family through hell, and the best you can do is try to fill his head with silly little Bible stories that many people think are barely one step up from fairy tales and get him to memorize boring Scripture verses that he can't even understand by treating him like a puppy and rewarding him with a stupid trinket? That's the most ridiculous thing I've ever heard of. But go ahead and do it, because I'll have him for lunch."

It does seem like a silly way to prepare a boy for battle.

WHEN THE LIGHTS COME ON

But here is where I want every Sunday school teacher to pay close attention. Yes, the Evil One laughs. And the world laughs. And even some in the church snicker at your efforts, which seem so meager and, from the grand perspective of life, so insignificant. But this is one of those places where God uses the foolish things of the world to confound the wise.

God uses the "joke" of Sunday school to implant something profoundly powerful and far-reaching into the mind of that little boy. Yes, the little boy named Billy, the one who once took glue and pasted the flannel graph onto the flannel board. Yes, the one who placed thumbtacks on every seat in the third-grade Sunday school class in hopes that someone would sit down on one. Yes, the one who spent the better part of fifth- and sixth-grade Sunday school in the "mine shaft" (a dark closet) because he couldn't keep his mouth shut. Yes, the one who in seventh grade led the boys in his class to so terrorize the brand-new teacher that the man failed to return the following Sunday. Yes, little Billy, the very one who treated Sunday school about as lightheartedly as anyone ever did.

Hard as it may be to believe, God used the "joke" of Sunday school to prepare little Billy for battle. Because the truths that floated up into my consciousness at the critical moments did not come from nowhere. They were born of seeds planted way back in Sunday school, when I wasn't even paying attention.

So I say to every Sunday school teacher: your task is not

a joke. Don't ever be deceived into disparaging it. You'll probably never get glory for it. You'll probably never even find out how life turns out for the kids you work with. But I tell you that what may appear to be a foolish task is no less than the beginning of wisdom and the hope that a little boy or girl may receive light someday when they grow up and find themselves in a dark place.

When I found myself in a dark place, those little lights began to come on. At first, I didn't pay much attention to them. They were like fireflies flickering for an instant, then disappearing into the darkness. But as I experienced those moments of awareness again and again over quite a long time, I became more conscious of their happening. And I began to realize that I was not just remembering truth; I was *experiencing* truth.

I'm not saying you have to have grown up in a good Sunday school program to experience truth. God has all kinds of ways to "turn the lights on" for people, so to speak. So don't fret if you come from a very different background. I'm just saying that in my case I came to the time of trial with a head full of Bible verses, but I didn't appreciate their value until the fighting began.

To use a different analogy, it was a bit like working a crossword puzzle (which, to be honest, I've never done very much, even though I do pretty well with words; Nancy, on the other hand, worked on the *New York Times* puzzle every day, right up to the end of her life).

The things I learned in Sunday school and growing up in my family were like the numbered clues of the puzzle. Those were the givens. Then, as I worked my way through the experience of the past ten years, I began to fill in the blanks of the puzzle, guided by the clues. At different moments I was able to say, "Oh, *that's* what that means." Or, "Hmm, now I see." Or "Wow! I hadn't seen that, but that makes perfect sense."

Over the course of ten years, I filled in quite a bit of the puzzle. And in that way I came to realize that what God had said about the nature of reality is true. Indeed, it is more true than I had realized, and true in ways that I hadn't realized.

Not to put words in God's mouth, but it was as if He were saying, "Hey, Bill! I told you—all of you there on planet Earth—it would be this way. I told you from the outset what would happen. I didn't pull any punches. I told you straight-out that you would know good and evil. And now you can see I wasn't lying. I told you the truth."

And that, my friend, was and is a great comfort. Yes, the truth about this world may be an awful truth. So awful, in fact, that we have no appreciation for how true and awful it is until we find ourselves right smack in the teeth of it, so that our experience, which is undeniable, confirms what God has said.

That truth may be an awful truth. But it is a great comfort to know that it is true, nonetheless. And here's why: *because if what God has declared about evil is true, then what He has declared about Himself must be just as true.* If I discover that He is absolutely right about the bad news, then why should I not believe that He is absolutely right about the good news as well?

And at some point, all of us in the House of Mourning are hoping and praying that we'll hear some good news. Well, here we are.

EIGHT

"Come Forth!"

The good news is that Jesus wept.

That's right! For people in the House of Mourning, a great deal of the good news for which we hope and pray is to be found in the shortest verse in the Bible: "Jesus wept."[1] Indeed, those two words turn out to be *great* news for anyone who feels betrayed by God. And I have a pretty good feeling that many reading this book have felt betrayed by God.

I say that because even some of Jesus's best friends felt betrayed by Him. Perhaps none more than the three siblings Lazarus, Martha, and Mary. According to the Gospels, few were closer to Jesus than these three. They were so close that they let Jesus come and go to their home in Bethany, near Jerusalem, as if He were one of the family.

One day Lazarus fell ill with what appeared to be a terminal illness. Most of us turn to God in prayer at a time like that. And that's what Lazarus, Martha, and Mary did. Except, instead of praying, all they had to do was send word to Jesus. After all, He was one of their best friends. Talk about firsthand access to divine power!

Their message was the sort of brief, urgent word that family use with one another: "Lord, the one you love is sick."[2] I like how they put that. "Lord, the one *you love* is sick." Not just, "Lazarus is sick," but "Your friend, the man You care about, the man You love like a brother, the man You stay up late at night with to talk after everyone else has gone home or gone to sleep, the man who lets You sit in his favorite chair when You teach—Lord, *that* man is sick. *Your friend.* He's dying. He needs You. Come quickly!" It was the request of people who knew they could count on their special friend, Jesus.

As soon as that request reached Jesus, He . . . stayed put. Did nothing. Just kept on doing whatever it was He was doing. Some friend, huh?

Then finally Lazarus died. Can you imagine the impact that moment must have had on those two sisters? I know that when I watched Nancy take her very last breath and felt her utterly limp hand in mine, my whole world changed. I will never view life the same again. Ever. For seven years, we and countless others had prayed. Early on, we prayed for healing. Later on, we prayed for time. Nancy's prayer was never for a miracle, only that she be allowed to watch her girls grow up.

Whatever our prayers, Nancy died anyway. And if, as I've indicated earlier, I wondered at times whether my prayers were even heard, I could always chalk it up to some deficiency in me—some lack of faith, perhaps, or a heart not quite right with God.

"IF YOU HAD BEEN HERE. . ."

But Martha and Mary *knew* that their request had been heard by Jesus. They also *knew* that He was quite capable of healing diseases. So the fact that Jesus didn't show up in time was not due to their lack of faith or inadequacies in asking. They waited for Jesus—and Jesus simply didn't show up! In fact, He didn't even show up at the funeral. Some friend, huh?

> The first casualty of suffering is trust.

No wonder, then, that when Jesus finally did appear, four days later, both of the grieving sisters said the same thing: "Lord, if you had been here, my brother would not have died." Implication: You let us down.[3]

I am certain that many who are reading this book feel let down by God. In their own way they are saying, "Lord, if You had been here, my husband would not have died." "Lord, if You had been here, my daughter wouldn't have been the passenger in that car." "Lord, if You had been here, my toddler would not have fallen into that swimming pool." "Lord, if You had been here, my baby would not have miscarried." "Lord, if You had been here. . . But You weren't. You let me down."

The saying goes that the first casualty of war is truth. Well, the first casualty of suffering is trust. When something bad has happened to us, it's instinctive to start asking, where was God? It's the feeling of betrayal.

I believe Martha and Mary felt completely betrayed by Jesus. A conflicted feeling of betrayal, no doubt. On the one hand, the fact that Jesus was a no-show was undeniable. That had to raise doubts: What's the deal? Where have You been? Why didn't You come? How could You do this to us?

Even when we have the greatest reason to doubt, we don't *want* to doubt.

But on the other hand, they could not totally abandon all trust in Jesus, because, after all, they knew by experience that Jesus was trustworthy, that Jesus was kind, that Jesus had integrity, that Jesus cared about them and their brother. Sure, they may have felt deeply hurt by His absence, but they could not just give up on Him. They knew Him to be someone who would *not*, in fact, let them and their brother down. So what were they supposed to think?

A lot of us today feel similarly conflicted about Jesus. On the one hand, He seems to remain silent just when we need Him most. So we feel hurt or angry or disappointed or whatever. Yet despite our feelings, we can't quite bring ourselves to just throw our faith away and say, "Well, forget that! This whole Jesus thing was just a lot of foolishness. How could I have ever believed that?"

Oh, I suppose some people end up there. But I wonder if those people weren't just playing games to begin with and trying to use God the way I mentioned earlier, as a sort of wizard who can wave a wand and make their troubles disappear. Most of us who have ever made any honest attempt to stay in a relationship with God find that our faith is surprisingly stubborn. Even when we have the greatest reason to doubt, we don't *want* to doubt; we want to believe. We'd just like some tangible evidence from God's side of things to give our teetering faith a handhold before we fall off the cliff. And so we end up conflicted, just like Martha and Mary.

Martha and Mary provide two case studies in how conflicted people come to Jesus. Martha appears to have been furious with Him, and worked very hard to suppress her seething anger. Meanwhile, Mary's emotions were torn to shreds by just plain hurt. All she could do was fall down and sob at Jesus's feet.[4]

THE LAST THING WE'D EXPECT

In my life, I've approached Jesus with both anger and tears (among other emotions), and I have found that either approach can get His attention. But I think tears get to His heart faster. They certainly did in Mary's case: "When Jesus therefore saw her weeping, and the Jews who came with her, also weeping, He was deeply moved in spirit, and was troubled."[5]

Now that's a powerful statement. The One who told His disciples not to be "troubled"[6] was Himself "troubled." What must it have taken for the Lord of all to be distressed like that? Clearly, something profound was going on. And in that troubled, distressed state, Jesus asked to be taken to the grave of His friend. On the way, the account tells us, He wept.

Jesus wept.

I don't know what frame of mind you are in as you have picked up this book. But whatever your condition, I urge

you to focus your attention for a while on this curious incident when Jesus wept. I happen to believe it is among the
most important things He ever did for those of us in the
House of Mourning.

And yet I'm quite sure that tears were the last thing anyone expected from Jesus on that day in Bethany. Emotions
were running high, as they always do in a crisis. And everyone expected Jesus to *do* something or *say* something that
would somehow make amends for His appalling insensitivity
at not showing up in time. So as usual, when everyone expected something from Jesus, Jesus did something that no
one expected: He cried. I'd pay attention to that. Because
the fact that Jesus wept means He was human.

Nowadays, I run into a lot of people for whom Jesus is
not a man but a sort of superman. It's as if He could live
above this world rather than in this world. Yet the New Testament clearly teaches that He laid aside whatever advan-
tages He might have brought to the human experience.[7] His
tears are evidence of that. They show that He felt genuine
emotion, just as we do.

That is very good news for those of us in the House of
Mourning. It means that Jesus is here with us in our house of
pain. And He's here as a *human.* Same limitations. Same
troubles. Same emotions. Jesus is one of us.

Which suggests to me that when I turn to Jesus for help
and comfort in my time of trial, I should approach Him *first*
through His humanity, not His divinity. Indeed, I believe
that is what He Himself would prefer. Because that is the way
He related to Martha and Mary and the friends and neighbors of Lazarus. As a human *first,* and only later on as God.

THE COMFORT OF JESUS'S TEARS

If you read the story in John 11, you'll see that most everyone in the situation was focused on Jesus's divinity.[8] But Jesus was in a completely different place. Oh, yes, He was the Son of God, as He would shortly demonstrate. But on the way to the tomb, He did the most human thing there is: He wept.

Crying is about losing emotional control. I admit it's a bit shocking to think that Jesus lost emotional control. But unless you're willing to believe that His tears were just putting on an act for the crowd, you have to conclude that as He walked to Lazarus's tomb, Jesus came apart emotionally in much the same way that Martha and Mary and their friends were coming apart.

I find that oddly reassuring. That says to me that Jesus was alive. He was a real, live human. He, too, lived in a fallen world where bad stuff happens, and life sometimes kicks you in the teeth, and people you love die. And when that happened, He cried. Just like you and me.

> You may be like me in that you keep wanting Jesus to do the "God thing," the miracle thing, the redemptive thing, the turnaround thing, the "rescue-me" thing.

At least, I hope it's like you and me. I know I cry. I hope you do, too. If you haven't cried in the face of whatever sorrow you've experienced, I have to wonder if you're alive. If you've never allowed yourself to feel the hurt, so that the tears well up and your throat catches and your mind kind of goes all muddy as thought and logic give way to pain and grief—are you sure your humanity is still active?

I worry about people in grief, because death can be sort of infectious, and some who live through the death of a loved one actually begin to die inside because they never let their humanity take the blow of the loss. Oh, they may remain quite functional. The question is whether they are still *alive,* because they have lost the capacity to feel.

Jesus felt the blow of Lazarus's death. He heard Mary's sobbing. He heard the mourners around Him wailing. He started the walk that would lead to the tomb holding the dead body of His friend. And thank God, rather than being strong in that moment, He let Himself be weak, and He broke down and cried with them all.

And with you and me. The fact that Jesus entered into Martha and Mary's pain provides strong evidence that He enters into our pain, as well. He meets us at our point of vulnerability, our humanity. And He doesn't *say* anything. At first, anyway. He just hears our crying, and next thing we know He is crying, too.

Through that I discover that the first thing I need in my grief is not Jesus as God but Jesus as human being. In my weakest condition, having lost emotional control, coming apart, I find Jesus coming alongside me in weakness, too, having lost emotional control and coming apart as He allows Himself to experience my pain, so that it is now His pain, too. That is profoundly comforting.

You see, you may be like me in that you keep wanting Jesus to do the "God thing," the miracle thing, the redemptive thing, the turnaround thing, the "rescue-me" thing—all the things I can't do, being human. I want Him to "fix" whatever it is that needs fixing. "Just do Your supernatural thing, Lord," is more or less my prayer. Which puts me in the same camp as the crowd at Bethany: "Could not this man, who opened the eyes of him who was blind, have kept this man also from dying?"[9]

I'm all focused on Jesus's power and authority as God. And so I pray, "Lord, be God for me!" And it's as if the Lord replies, "We'll get to that, Bill. I'll be God for you soon enough. But first, let Me be a human to you." And then when I look at Him, and the more I look at Him, the more I realize that His eyes are filled with tears. For me.

And when you're crying, can there be any greater comfort than to realize that Jesus Himself is crying along with you? That doesn't take the pain away; but it can make you adequate to the pain to know that Jesus is with you in the pain, so that it is now His pain, too.

THE TEARS OF GOD

But now let me suggest that the tears of Jesus were not only the tears of a man but the tears of God, as well. Because, of course, the wonderful thing about Jesus is that He *is* more than just another human. He is God. Ironically, I think that actually made Him feel *worse* about Lazarus's death than either the sisters or their community. Or even Lazarus.

I submit that Jesus, being God, ached with a conflict that only God could feel. He knew that He had the power to prevent Lazarus from dying. But for reasons known only to Him and His Father, He did not intervene before Lazarus died.

That must have hurt. It doesn't matter if Jesus already knew He was going to raise Lazarus from the dead. To have put His friend through death, and the sisters through loss, and the community through suffering, and His own self through grief. I could understand if Jesus felt that in some sense He *had* betrayed everyone. And I can imagine that even He might be asking, "Why does it have to be this way?"

Why does anyone have to die? The Christian answer is pretty brutal: because that is the ordained outcome for everyone living in this fallen world. That is the judgment. God warned that if we ate from the tree, we would die.[10] We ate. Now the consequence is unavoidable. God imposes death. It is certainly not what He intended. He intended life. But death now comes to every human being.[11] The man Jesus included.

Jesus hated the fact that anyone must die even more than we do. So His tears at Lazarus's tomb must have been to some degree an expression of divine grief over the human condition. A tremendous sorrow that creatures who were made for life should ever have to experience death. Even knowing that a resurrection was only minutes away, Jesus cried at a tomb.

That's an amazing thing to me—that God would shed tears. But then, how could He not shed tears? *Because His lovingkindness is everlasting.* Yes, God has pledged Himself— His own *Self*—permanently, always, without retreat, without reservation, without condemnation, with full power and authority to do so—God has pledged His life and His blood to faithfully, mercifully, and devotedly bring about His good on our behalf, in ways that vindicate us over evil. That is the passionate, virtually irrational commitment of His heart to us. His blood for our blood, His life for our life. Do you think a God who cares that much would remain dispassionate when we humans return to dust? Not a chance!

Of course, I doubt that Martha and Mary and the rest of the folks in Bethany were thinking about any of these things as they came to Lazarus's tomb. By that point they had given up hope. All they could do was stand there and cry, mourning the fact that Lazarus was gone. Sure, they'd see him again someday in heaven. But what comfort was that for such a huge loss? Especially when it could have been prevented—if only their Friend had shown up.

JESUS TAKES CONTROL

So, as always, we come back to the question, where is God? This time, though, we get an answer to that question. The answer is Jesus. There He is! There's God. In Jesus, God followed through on His promise to come after us. And what happened next in the Lazarus story is a powerful demonstration of God coming after us. Having shed His tears, Jesus composed Himself, took control, and did the second thing that no one expected Him to do that day. "Remove the stone," He told them.

Under the circumstances, the order not only violated custom; it seemed downright cruel. Why not leave the dead in peace? Because God doesn't leave dead people in peace! Not the ones who are His, anyway.

So they pried open the tomb, and nothing stood between Jesus and a dead body. It was then that He cried out in a loud voice, "Lazarus, come forth!"[12] It was not the volume of Jesus's voice that mattered. It was the authority behind the voice. As God, Jesus has the authority to restore life.

And so "he who had died came forth."[13] I like the way the text puts that. Not "Lazarus came forth," but he "*who had died* came forth." The author hammers home the fact that Lazarus really was dead. Which means that Jesus really did raise him from the dead.

And the reason Jesus raised Lazarus from the dead was not to prove that He was God, but *because* He was God. Being God, Jesus had a promise to fulfill—the promise of His lovingkindness. By raising Lazarus, Jesus was telling Martha and Mary and the people in Bethany and all the rest of us, "Never doubt! Never doubt! It's not a question of whether I *can* do it. That's a given. The issue is I *must* do it. I *must* raise you up. Because that is the pledge of my lovingkindness. To not leave you in the grave. You *are* going to die. That cannot be changed. But I will go after you there and bring you back. Because My lovingkindness is everlasting. It *never* dies."

Nancy believed in that resurrection. In her Bible, she underlined the following words: "He who raised Christ Jesus from the dead will also give life to your mortal bodies through His Spirit who indwells you."[14] Out to the side of that passage, she wrote: "PROMISE." And I know, because I was there, that she died with a pure, childlike trust in God to follow through on that promise.

Later, at Nancy's memorial service, we recited the Apostles' Creed, which ends with the words, "I believe in . . . the resurrection of the body; and the life everlasting." I said those words with full conviction, and concluded with a bold "Amen!" Like Nancy, I knew I believed firmly in the resurrection.

But as always, sometimes you don't know what you don't know.

THE ENCOUNTER IN MY KITCHEN

One morning as I was coming up on the first anniversary of Nancy's death, I was in the kitchen going through my usual ritual of packing lunches for the girls before they went off to school. I was standing at the counter, three sets of bread slices laid out in front of me. One for smoked turkey, one for roast beef, one for PB&J.

I wasn't thinking about anything in particular. I was just a single-parent dad, doing what you have to do to get three girls out the door and putting a house back in order before heading off to work. So I was spreading mayo when . . .

"He's alive, you know!"

Those words suddenly *expressed* themselves in my head. It wasn't a voice, but it might as well have been. The message was clear, unmistakable, unequivocal. Not just a thought. More like a presence. A single, brief statement that was as clear as a bell.

"He's alive, you know!"

The words just intruded. Unasked for, unprovoked, unexpected, undeniable, and unexplainable. They were just suddenly there. Inside me. And there was no question in my mind what—or who—they were referring to. They were re-ferring to Jesus.

I stopped slathering mayo for a moment, puzzled as to what had just happened, and wondering what to do with it. I mean, I've known my whole life about Jesus rising from the dead. Remember, I've been going to Sunday school since be-fore I was born. So the doctrine of Christ's resurrection was basic stuff for me. In truth, I was probably no more than five by the time I had that Apostles' Creed down cold: "The third day He arose again from the dead."

So I was mystified as to why those words had suddenly barged into my morning routine: "He's alive, you know!" Of course I knew that.

I moved on to putting the meat on the sandwiches and the jelly on the peanut butter. But you know, you can't just brush off something as odd as having a sudden strong aware-ness that Jesus is alive.

What came to me as I continued working was a mental image of Jesus's passion. I thought about His mistreatment, the injustice of His trial, the long road to Calvary, the pain of His ordeal. Mind you, this was two and a half years before Mel Gibson's movie. And it wasn't like I was seeing graphic images of brutality in my mind. Just a quiet awareness of Jesus's suffering. And the thought that kept coming to me again and again: *That was so unfair. No one should have to go through that.* I was feeling rather sad. Feeling sad, and then my mind drifting back to those words: *"He's alive, you know!"*

Instantly the sadness stopped! It just ended. Suddenly—it was gone! And what took its place was a picture in my mind of Jesus, alive and smiling and out of pain and happy. Yes, He had suffered. Yes, He had died a painful death. Yes, it was unfair. Yes, no one should have to go through that. But He did go through it. And now He was past it. He was out of the pain and suffering. He was *alive*—at that very moment. More alive than He had ever been before.

"Wow! He's alive!" I said to myself. "He really is alive."

The assertion was not so much a truth that I had come to—having, as I say, known the doctrine all my life. It was more like a truth that I was somehow experiencing, or certifying, if that makes sense.

Well, now I *really* had a lot to ponder. I liked the thought that Jesus is alive. But what did all of this mean?

Very little time had elapsed. In truth, I probably hadn't gotten beyond bagging the sandwiches and cutting a couple of tomato slices for Kristin.

My thoughts drifted to Nancy. I kind of pictured her, in my mind, there in the hospital during her last days. I won't go into detail as to what I recalled, but I will tell you that I saw her in suffering. I saw her in pain. And I was thinking, *She shouldn't have had to go through that. That wasn't fair. That wasn't right. No woman should have to go through that.*

And at that very moment my mind brought back that picture of Jesus, smiling and happy and out of pain and more alive than ever. And with that, another certainty took hold inside me: "Wow! Nancy is alive too! Nancy is there. With Jesus. Alive. It's true she suffered; it's true she died a painful death. And you're right, Bill, it wasn't fair, and no one should have to go through that. But she did go through it, and now she's past it. And she's with Jesus. He's raised her up! She's smiling and happy and out of pain and more alive than ever."

With that, the oddest thing of the whole, odd experience happened. The instant I realized that Nancy was out of suffering and with the Lord, I had the sensation of a great weight suddenly rolling off my shoulders and back. And I . . . well, I "came to," if you will. It was like having been trapped underwater for so long that you've run out of air. Then suddenly you find yourself free and breaking up through the surface of the water, and you suck in oxygen. That's what I did. I literally shook my head and took in deep gulps of air.

As I stood there, panting, I could now see that for the entire previous year I had been carrying around with me a mental image of Nancy in her last days in the hospital, suffering and in pain. That's how I had been remembering her. All year, I had been filtering my thoughts of Nancy through the lens of her suffering. And of course, that had translated into a tremendous heaviness in my heart, with feelings of sadness, disappointment, defeat, and resignation. That weight had been there for a year, but I hadn't realized it until that moment.

FILLED WITH LIGHT

So when that heaviness suddenly rolled off of me, it was like I'd been let go. Freed! Indeed, I felt a huge surge of energy release inside me, energy that had been absent for longer than I could remember. So much energy that I probably got more accomplished in the next three months than I had accomplished in the entire previous year.

Meanwhile, that old image of the suffering Nancy had

been replaced by a new one: I could see her alive and happy and out of pain and (most importantly) with her Lord. She was past the bad stuff. She was happier now than she had ever been. She was, in short, raised up with Christ. He had kept His promise. Her trust had been rewarded.

As this event came to its conclusion, I just stopped what I was doing. I stood there at the counter, wondering, *Did what I think just happened really happen?*

I looked around. No one else was there. Amy was in the living room practicing her violin. Kristin and Brittany were in their rooms. Kasey, our Australian shepherd, lay as usual with her nose on her bowl, trying to decide whether to get around to eating her dog food. Everything was as it had been.

Everything, that is, except me. I was . . . filled with light, is how I would put it. Breathing in light, like pure oxygen. Just brimming with energy. Lighthearted and blinking with amazement, not quite certain what had just occurred but knowing that I was feeling utterly invigorated as a result.

> If we ever need God, we certainly need Him after we're dead and gone.

Now I have to tell you that I thought twice, and twice again, before telling you about this incident. Because I know I run the risk of being misunderstood. Some people will read this story and think, *Bill really is playing mind games with himself.*

I've wondered about that myself—whether my mind was just playing tricks on me. I guess it's possible. I've certainly encountered people in mourning who have twisted reality all out of shape in order to make their situation more en-durable. But people who do that generally seem to be in de-nial and unwilling to accept their pain. I leave it to the reader to pass judgment on whether I'm in denial about my loss and unwilling to accept pain!

Another hesitation I had about including this admittedly extraordinary story is that some readers may think I am somehow embracing a mystical approach to God, based on subjective experience. Anyone who thinks that simply doesn't know me. Indeed, if you phoned up my therapist, I think he'd say that I could stand to have more spontaneous, mystical experiences. Because I do approach my life—and my faith—with both feet planted firmly on firm ground.

THE LIGHT THAT NEVER DIES

In short, I wouldn't waste too much time trying to figure out what provoked my experience at the kitchen counter. The thing to pay attention to is the truth that gripped me because of that experience—that God's lovingkindness extends all the way to the grave. If we ever need God, we certainly need Him after we're dead and gone, after we've died whatever death God has ordained for us to die. After He imposes His in-evitable judgment and we return to dust. After it appears that all is finished. At that ultimate point, when all that's left is a dead body, God shows up at our final resting place and in a loud voice cries out our name (because if we belong to Him, He knows our name): "Lazarus, come forth!" "Nancy, come forth!" "Bill, come forth!" "My child, come forth!"

That's the truth that my experience that morning pointed

me back to. That Jesus really is the resurrection and the life. That after He cries over the death of His friends, He doesn't leave them dead but raises them up, as the creed says, to "life everlasting." Because His lovingkindness is everlasting. It just doesn't go away. It never has. It never will.

The enemy of our souls never understood that. It never occurred to him that God would climb into this evil, fallen world *with* us and subject Himself to the same evil, the same judgment, and ultimately the same death. It never dawned on him that even before God made us, He swore Himself to our good. Before He ever gave us hearts of our own, He gave His own heart to us. His blood for our blood, His life for our life.

And so when we're in trouble, and our trust is wavering, and we find ourselves asking, where is God? we need to realize that God is *right here with us.* Right here in the big mess of a fallen world. Right here in the darkness with us. Right here in the emergency room with us. Right here at the bedside with us. Right here at the graveside with us. Right here in the grief with us. Right here on the cross with us, crying out the same pain we cry: "My God, My God, why have you forsaken Me? Where are you? Where are you, Father? Where are you when I need you?" He feels that same sense of being cut off and on His own.

And then . . . He even goes into the grave with us. And *for* us. In short, God's lovingkindness takes Him all the way to the worst depths to which our fallenness subjects us.

Having come to us there, He asks a central question— the ultimate question—of *trust.* In effect He says, "You've asked Me where I am, and here I am—right here with you in your mess. I said I'd come—that's what my lovingkindness is all about. Well, here I am. So if I've lived up to My word this far, can you trust Me to follow through on the rest of what I've said I'll do? Can you trust Me to find the way out of this mess?"

I do. Over the last ten years, I have found God to be utterly trustworthy. Somehow, during my stay at the House of Mourning, all the truths I've ever known about God have become more true than I'd ever imagined, and true in ways that I hadn't even seen.

Make no mistake. Nancy's death has hurt more than I have described. Nor does the hurt just go away. But I'll say this: God has shown up for me, as He did for her, and for my daughters.

This is not a pretend thing, or a mind game I play to comfort myself. I would simply be a dishonest person if I didn't say plainly and openly that I have found God to be utterly trustworthy in the worst moment that life has yet thrown at me.

NINE

The Power of Presence

I have a hunch and a hope that some readers have picked up this book, not because they themselves are in the House of Mourning but because someone they know and care about is in the House of Mourning. If you are one of those readers, this chapter is for you.

Perhaps your interest is professional, in that you frequently encounter death and dying in your role as pastor, counselor, psychologist, physician, nurse, paramedic, police officer, or teacher. Or your connection may be personal, in that you are a friend or acquaintance to someone in your church, at work, in your neighborhood, or somewhere else in your world who is experiencing grief and loss and suffering. Either way, let me say a brief word to those who stand by as someone they care about goes through his or her sorrow.

First, a disclaimer. This chapter is not intended to be a

primer on grief recovery or a manual on pastoral care. I am not a professional in such matters, just someone who has been through and continues to go through his own (limited) experience, and who is offering his own (limited) perspective based on that experience. Experts who are trained to deal with people like me will no doubt have a lot to add to—and perhaps even subtract from—what I suggest here.

I said early on that I've learned three things in the House of Mourning. The first thing is that evil is real. The second thing is that if what God has declared about evil is true, then what He has declared about Himself must be just as true. And what is that? That His lovingkindness is everlasting. I have found that to be a true statement. I can trust that.

So now the third thing I've learned is this: in moments of grief and pain and suffering, the lovingkindness of God is best expressed in emotions and actions, not theology or philosophy.

Please understand, I have nothing against theology or philosophy. But it's an issue of using the right tools for the job. When it comes to grief and loss, the tools of logic and reason may be among the worst to use, because instead of alleviating a person's suffering, they may inadvertently add to it.

What is grief? What is loss? Whatever else, they are traumas that one *experiences*. There's your key to the nature of the task. Mourning is not a rational exercise. People don't *think* their way into it. Something bad happens, and they find themselves there. It's something a person *experiences*. That being the case, it follows that when it comes to grief and loss, God's lovingkindness must be *experienced*.

How does that happen? Through people. Lovingkindness

becomes incarnational. It's not a concept, it's a person. The first person was Jesus. He is the supreme expression of God's lovingkindness. As I pointed out in the previous chapter, He climbed into this fallen world with us, and went all the way to the worst depths to which our fallenness subjects us. When Jesus showed up, God showed up for us.

He still does—through people, particularly those who have themselves experienced His lovingkindness.

THE PIE—AND THE PERSON

During the summer before she died, Nancy had to go into the hospital. By that point, the girls and I had become fairly used to rearranging our lives to accommodate the ups and downs of a parent with cancer. Still, we certainly had our hands full trying to get along without Mommy. And I was especially feeling the stress of responsibility bearing down on me, such that even little provocations felt like huge impositions.

In that frame of mind, I heard the doorbell ring one evening as I was trying to throw a meal together. *Now what?* I thought to myself. None of the girls was immediately available to answer the door. So it was up to me to drop what I was doing and go find out who had chosen to invade our lives at this particular, untimely moment. (You can see I was prepared to be Mr. Hospitality.)

I opened the door expecting to see one of the girls' friends. Instead, I was greeted by a face that I had not seen in probably thirty years. As soon as that face saw me, it brightened into the kindest, most compassionate smile I may have ever seen. Certainly the kindest, most compassionate smile I had seen that day.

"Bill, I don't know if you remember me, but my name is Ann Haughton. I'm now Ann _____. I live not too far away. I heard your wife went into the hospital, and I just wanted to drop this off for your family." With that she handed over a pie that was still warm from the oven.

> Out of the blue, she had made an effort to reach out and show a kindness to a friend in need, even though she had not seen him in thirty years.

Very surprised by this totally unexpected visit, I invited her to stay a moment and catch up, but she had left her car running, and she said she knew I was probably fixing dinner. So after exchanging the briefest of pleasantries, we said good-bye and she was gone.

Now it's interesting to me that this simple incident should stand out in my memory. I mean, sure, the pie was a kind gesture and all. But in truth, so many people showed up with so much food in the years before Nancy died—as well as for months after she died—that we probably still have remnants of it stored in my mom's freezer. So in truth, there was nothing remarkable about another pie coming in the door.

But it wasn't the pie that made the impact. It was the person. During the summers of my high school years, I had worked at Pine Cove, a camp and conference center just getting started near Tyler, Texas. One of the first families to bring their kids to Pine Cove was the Haughtons. They had four girls. Ann was the oldest, and she ended up working on staff a couple of those summers while I was there.

Teens learn a lot about each other when they work long hours side by side over the course of a Texas summer. They learn which ones are the contenders and which ones are the pretenders. I came to know Ann as a true contender. She always struck me as reliable and steadfast, a girl with a level head, and someone you could count on when the chips were down. Indeed, if you knew you were headed into a situation where there was liable to be trouble, Ann would be someone you'd want to have on your team.

Eventually, I lost touch with Ann and her family. After Nancy and I moved to Dallas, I occasionally heard the family name and would remember them. But for thirty years our paths never crossed.

Until Ann showed up at my door that evening. Under the circumstances, she didn't have to do anything. I would have never known. But for me, on that night, God used Ann to extend His lovingkindness. Yes, through a gesture as unbelievably simple as a pie.

You see, I knew something about the person who had made that pie. She was that person you could count on in a time of trouble. And so I had an inkling as to what may have motivated her to bake a pie. It didn't matter that she hadn't talked to me in thirty years. Once she heard about my wife's situation, she felt compelled to do something to let me know I wasn't alone. Something very simple but very profound. She wasn't trying to fix my situation. She couldn't do that. But she was being there for me. And with me.

"I WILL GET YOU THROUGH THIS"

Ann's small gesture made a big difference. As I closed the door and returned to the kitchen, my mood was considerably brighter. I felt humbled and grateful. And I slowly realized that God was saying, "Bill, never forget: I'm here for you. I'm with you. You are not alone. I will get you through this." And with that, I finished fixing dinner. And, for the record, we did enjoy the pie for dessert!

The person in pain needs our tears more than our words.

The New Testament calls people like Ann, who are followers of Jesus, His "body." And for good reason. Like a body, Christans are expressions and extensions of Jesus. We express and extend God's lovingkindness into the world. Sometimes that lovingkindness means working on a Habitat for Humanity house. Sometimes it means teaching a Sunday school class to miscreant boys like little Billy. Sometimes it means sending a check to World Vision or the Salvation Army or your church. Sometimes it means sitting down with your neighbor or coworker and having a meaningful talk about life and eternity and what this "Jesus thing" is all about.

But of course, inevitably it happens. The bad stuff happens. We get an e-mail from a friend saying that he's just been diagnosed with cancer. We get a phone call from someone who says, "Did you hear about Jill? She passed away in her sleep last night." We get a note from the principal's office saying one of our students won't be in class today; his brother died in a car crash on the way to school. We greet someone at church, and she informs us, "Rod won't be here today. His mother died of a heart attack." We sit with a friend in a waiting room, and the surgeon comes through the doors, saying, "I'm sorry."

Most of us standing by at that awful, awkward moment have the same reaction: "I don't know what to say."

May I make an observation? It seems to me that if words were the most important thing people needed when bad stuff happens, then God would have created us human beings to be at our most eloquent when tragedy strikes. But the fact that we almost always *don't* know what to say is a pretty good indication that words are not called for at such a time. Something else is in order.

I'm not saying that words are unimportant. They can be vitally important. But it's a matter of timing—and, of course, one's choice of words when the time comes to say something. But in my experience, the verbal usually needs to be preceded by the nonverbal.

And so the person or family in pain needs our tears more than our words. Our hugs more than our advice. Our smiles more than our help. Our presence more than our perspective. Our silence even more than our prayers. They need us to just "be." And to let the person in pain "be" and feel whatever they "be" and feel. Is that so hard?

Actually, yes. It can be especially hard if you're among those who get paid to say things: clergy, counselors, CEOs, or parents, teachers, and others in leadership roles. And it can be unbearably hard if you are gifted with eloquence, and always have powerful, impactful, or wise things to say. When trouble strikes, your natural impulse is to say things. But I say, resist that impulse! The time for words will come, and at that time, you will earn your keep. But remember what I said in an earlier chapter: it is not that what you have to say is unimportant, but that the person is probably unable to hear it. Because they are not listening with their ears or their mind, but with their heart.

THE IMPORTANCE OF BEING-WITH

When Nancy began to experience significant pain at the end of her life, the doctors gave her morphine. The drug had a come-and-go effect on her, causing her to occasionally drift off in mid-sentence, as if sleeping. Then, with a start, she would come to and pick up where she had left off. Needless to say, communicating with her became more and more of a challenge.

His willingness to just be with her meant more than any profound answers he could have offered concerning God's omnipotence.

One day as Nancy was in this condition, our pastor, Skip Ryan, stopped by her hospital room for a visit. As he sat with Nancy for a while, one thing I appreciated was that he hadn't brought any prescripted sermonettes to give her. Instead, he let her control the conversation. Finally he said, "Nancy, I have to leave in a moment. But before I go, are there any questions I can answer while I'm here?"

To my surprise, Nancy nodded. Then, slowly and with

great difficulty because of the oxygen tube and the morphine and her efforts to breathe, she began to speak. "I was wondering. Is God able . . . ?" And with that, she drifted off.

Skip and I glanced at each other and shrugged. Neither of us said anything. We just waited for her to "come back." After a moment, she did, and then looked at Skip as if for an answer to a fully framed question. With a very gracious and understanding smile, he said, "Nancy, you began to ask me if God is able to do something, and I'm not sure I caught what it is you want to know that He can do. Do you remember?"

She looked puzzled and finally shook her head.

"Well," Skip went on, "whatever it was, I think the answer is *yes*." He then read her a relevant passage of Scripture. Nancy nodded and smiled ever so slightly. And then I think she nodded off again. When she came to, Skip prayed with her before leaving. And then he was gone.

The visit was a great comfort to Nancy, and to me. And what made an even greater impact than Skip as a pastor was Skip as a person. His willingness to just be with her, as she fought her battle—which was spiritual as well as physical— meant more than any profound answers he could have offered concerning God's omnipotence.[1]

Does that seem too easy—to just "be" with someone in their suffering? Does it seem like something you wouldn't want to do, because almost anyone could do it? Well here is a mystery: it's true that almost anyone could do it; so then why are there so few who do?

Nancy's room was on a floor of the hospital where, I discovered, they place the terminal cases. During the ten days that she was there, I took walks up and down the corridors of that floor. What struck me over time was how many of those people never had any visitors. I mean, with the exception of the medical personnel and the hospital chaplain, some who were there had *no one* to be with them in their final days and hours.

I'm sure that many of them were reaping the bitter consequences of having burned their relationships with family or friends. But how sad can it be to come down to the last of your life, wasting away in a hospital room, with no one who cares about you enough to stop by and just sit with you as you come to the end? I can assure you that when that time comes, you're not looking for anything profound; you just want a person to be with you and provide a human touch.

Or, to look at it another way, to provide God's touch. And God's presence. Because many of those lonely people living out their last hours are lying there with one question gnawing at their soul: Where is God? How special would it be to be the one that God sends as His answer to that desperate cry?

TAKING CARE OF BILL

Special, yes, but not necessarily pleasant. There's an emotional toll to watching someone die (remember, even Jesus wept). On the last day of Nancy's life, our longtime friends Bob and Jerrie Moffett happened to be flying from Boston to Phoenix with a connection through DFW Airport. Having been alerted to Nancy's situation, they arranged to lay over a few extra hours in order to take a cab from the airport to the hospital.

By the time they arrived, Nancy was very weak. I could

tell that it was heart-wrenching for the Moffetts to see one of their dearest friends suffering and literally within hours of dying. But for Nancy's sake, I'll be forever grateful that they stopped by. Who else would you want to show up for you at such a time than people who have proven their love time and again over many years? That was a hard thing to do. But it was a grace. It was a willingness to be God's presence.

I, too, was graced with the presence of people who were the hands and feet of God for me—though I did not always recognize it at the time. One of those people was Alex. I didn't meet Alex until Nancy had already gone metastatic. Which meant that by then most everyone's primary focus and energy, including mine, were devoted to Nancy. That was as it should be. But an unintended consequence of that was that my own needs were often neglected—most of all by me. We had a lot of people taking care of Nancy. Who was taking care of Bill?

Enter Alex. Not that he showed up in my life thinking, *I'm going to be Bill's support.* In truth, he came seeking help with his career. But the answer to the question, "Who is taking care of Bill?" is inevitably God. God knew what I needed. And God had given Alex a giftedness for making himself useful to people in unobtrusive ways. So when Alex realized that I was a man in significant trouble, he just started doing what God had naturally gifted him to do. Which was to just "be there" for Bill.

"Being there for Bill" took many forms. Lots of times we'd meet at a Starbucks. Alex always asked about Nancy, but he never tried to "get me to talk" about Nancy. That gave me a great deal of freedom in the relationship, and I will always be grateful for that. It meant that when I wanted to talk about the cancer, Alex would sit and listen. If I didn't want to talk about it, he didn't press it. We'd talk about other things.

And I needed to talk about "other things." Because if all I had talked about was cancer, I would have become completely dysfunctional. That's a real danger for individuals and their families when they face a life-threatening disease. The illness can become the center of gravity, such that everything in the home starts getting seen with respect to the illness, and the family and its members start getting defined in terms of the illness. Alex made it safe to talk about something besides cancer—without denying the cancer.

Alex also helped me stay tethered to some semblance of "normalcy" by occasionally pulling me out of the situation at home and doing utterly normal things. Like going to a movie or a ball game. Or going to Deep Ellum for Mexican food. Or going dove hunting. Or moving a refrigerator.

Sounds like Alex was just being a friend, you may be saying. Well, of course he was being a friend. But not "just" a friend. Let me put it this way: Alex felt a sense of calling in his relationship to me. I know that because he told me that. The more he realized what I was dealing with, the more compelled he felt to become intentional about paying attention to my welfare.

But not with a messiah complex. I know some people who respond to the notion of being God's person in a bad situation by trying to come in as the savior. They want to do spectacular things that impress everyone. They tend to want to take control. But all that does is divert energy and attention from where it's most needed—at the service of those in need. Alex never tried to be a savior for me. He tried to be a servant. Servants have a wonderful way of being invaluable when you need them and invisible when you don't need them. Alex had a genius for reading my needs and responding accordingly.

WHEN ONE SUFFERS . . .

Maybe the reason more of us don't show up with loving-kindness is because we are not in touch with our own feelings about pain and suffering and grief and loss and death. Some of us don't even want to be in touch with those feelings because, let's face it, they are not very pleasant feelings.

But as a Christian, am I not refusing to identify with Christ's body by not paying attention to the emotional impact our fallen world has on us? When the New Testament says that if one member of the body suffers, we all suffer, it is not stating an ideal, but a reality.[2] Think about it: when bad stuff happens to one of us, we all suffer because that tragedy slaps the rest of us in the face with the cold, brutal reality that evil is real. The evil falls on our brother or sister, but it sends a shudder through the rest of us as well. The question is, *Are we willing to feel that shudder and thereby identify with our suffering brother or sister?*

Tragedies test all of us—not just those directly involved, but also those of us who stand by with concern. So we do well to get honest and clean with our own emotions first. Otherwise, we cannot be of much use to those who are experiencing the suffering firsthand. Indeed, we actually become a burden to them, because now they have to take care of us.

Sooner or later, we're all going to get tested, because trouble is headed our way—either trouble of our own, or trouble for those we care about. It's just inevitable. In a fallen world, bad stuff is going to happen. When it does, the question is going to get asked: Where is God? In the last chapter, the answer to that question was Jesus.

But in this chapter, there's a second answer to that question. Or ought to be. The answer is *people*—particularly those of us who ourselves have been touched and transformed by God's lovingkindness.

This all sounds good, doesn't it? But does it really happen that way? Yes, actually it does. It has happened time and again for me. And on one occasion, it was one of my daughters who showed Nancy and me what God's lovingkindness looks like when clothed in nothing fancier than blue jeans, a T-shirt, and a sincere heart.

TEN

God
Shows Up

Never was a girl in love with the trumpet more than my daughter Brittany.

Traditionally the trumpet has been regarded as an instrument for boys, not girls. But Brittany has never paid much attention to what other people think. Once she decided she wanted to play the trumpet, the gender of the matter became irrelevant. And so, in fifth grade, Brittany devoted herself to the trumpet in the same way that she had devoted herself to previous interests in her life: with a laserlike focus and an all-consuming passion.

I remember when she brought the rented trumpet home from school. Utterly beside herself with excitement, she couldn't wait to take the instrument out of its case, show me its golden shine, and demonstrate how to hold it. Then, with a smile of utter confidence and delight, she brought the mouthpiece to her lips and blew into it with a flourish. A noise came out that sounded like a sick cow pleading to be put out of its misery.

Oh, man! I thought. *How am I ever going to live with this thing in the house?* But I wisely kept my mouth shut.

Nancy, who was much more understanding about the fact that we all have to start somewhere, began clapping enthusiastically, and the rest of us joined in. After a few more bleats, Brittany took a bow and the performance was over.

But the practicing went on night after night. Before long, there were concerts, and then chair tests, and then competitions. Brittany approached each one as if it were her own personal appearance at Carnegie Hall. She would drive herself to get the notes right. Over and over and over and over. Talk to herself. Urge herself on. Take a break. Back to it. Finally, her lip played out, she would give it a rest.

Personally I worried about her intensity at that age. I was afraid she might burn out. But it was a needless concern. Once she discovered how much fun it was to be a girl who could beat the boy trumpeters, nothing could stop her.

BRITTANY'S DREAM

By the eighth grade, it was obvious that Brittany had a future with the trumpet. She was the first trumpet in her school band. She was winning awards, taking private lessons, and looking toward high school when she would compete at the state level. Her eyes glowed with the prospect!

One day, in late spring of that year, she came to me and said, "Daddy, you know how I want to go to All-State Band next year?" Know? How could I not know? It was the only thing she'd talked about since Christmas.

"Yes," I replied matter-of-factly.

"Well, I've been thinking." When I heard that, I was pretty sure I was about to get hit up for some money. "If I'm going to be playing at that level—and you know, Mommy's been working on getting me lessons with Mr. Giangiulio—" (Rick Giangiulio was, at the time, the principal trumpet player with the Dallas Symphony, so "at that level" meant at the highest level) "then I'm going to need an upgrade on my trumpet."

Well, of course, you don't "upgrade" a trumpet the way you upgrade a computer. The child was talking about a new trumpet. "So what sort of trumpet do you have in mind?" I asked.

Asking Brittany a question like that is akin to asking Dale Earnhardt Jr. what sort of engine he needs to win the Daytona 500. You can rest assured that she had already researched every trumpet on the market in minute detail, had asked the advice of professionals, had pored over catalogs, had evaluated costs, had looked at the longer-term implications of owning this or that instrument, had considered resale value, and had digested maybe three million other data points to figure out which trumpet was *the* best choice for her.

"The Bach Stradivarius," she replied, without a moment's hesitation. "That's really the trumpet I need."

"What does Mommy say?"

"Well, she agrees with me that a Bach Stradivarius would be a really good trumpet to have."

"But I told her she would have to pay for part of it," Nancy interjected as she came into the room to join the conversation. Funny how that happened. The two of them looked at me as if to say, "Well, what are you waiting for?"

Brittany continued, "What I want to know is, how much you and Mommy are willing to pay, and how much do I have to come up with?"

"Well, how much are we talking about here?" I asked.

"I'd have to get an exact price," Brittany explained. "But a Bach Strad retails for around $2,500, maybe a little more. But I'm pretty sure Mr. Giangiulio can get me a good one for around $2,000."

"Two thousand dollars is a lot of money, Brittany." I've always been a master of the obvious.

"I know," she countered. "But I really need it, and I'll do whatever I have to do to earn my part." The last thing I was worried about was whether Brittany would do her part. Of course she would do her part. It was *my* part that had me concerned.

"Well, let me talk with Mommy about what we think we can afford," I told her.

"Thank you, Daddy!" she said with a big smile, and rushed from the room. I sat there feeling like a banker who'd just had his vault cleaned out by an inside job.

In the end, with Mr. Giangiulio's assistance, Brittany located a dealer who would sell her a brand, spankin' new Bach Stradavarius for $1,935. Nancy and I agreed to cover two-thirds of the cost, which left Brittany $645 to beg, borrow, or steal.

And so she did. She took on babysitting. She appealed to

friends and relatives for odd jobs like raking leaves, washing cars, cleaning windows, feeding pets. She stashed away her daily milk money into her trumpet fund. By the time school ended and she was preparing to go to camp, she had $450 saved up. Quite a sum!

But not quite enough.

"I've got until June 13," she said one day. "That's two weeks before Baylor Band Camp, and I *really* want that trumpet for band camp."

"I thought band camp wasn't until the end of June," I said.

"It isn't. But if I'm going to take a new trumpet to band camp, I've *got* to have it a couple weeks beforehand, so I can break it in and get used to it." Brittany was counting the days. "I've only got a little more than two weeks to find that money."

Well, we'll see, I thought to myself.

At the beginning of June, Nancy and I drove Brittany and Kristin to Pine Cove for a week of camp. I was happy that they could get a break from school and the city. I was even happier that Nancy could have a lighter week without the two older girls, to catch up on things she wanted to do. But, of course, I was most happy that I could have a week without the sound of a trumpet in the house at all hours.

And so we all had a great week. Then, on Saturday, we went and picked up the girls and heard stories and camp songs and skits and cheers all the way home.

"And guess what, Daddy?" Brittany exclaimed from the backseat. "You know that $50 that you and Mommy deposited for me at the snack shop? Well, I only used $5 of it. So that leaves $45 to go in the trumpet fund."

"Brittany!" I protested. "You shouldn't have done that. You were supposed to use that money to have fun."

"I know," she replied, "but I had lots of fun anyway, and now I have $495 for the trumpet. Only $150 to go!" She was so excited.

Both girls were emphatic that they'd never had a better week in their lives, and that even beyond the fun and the activities and the games and the rest, the thing they most liked about Pine Cove was how much closer it had brought them to God.

"I learned that I really need to trust God for things," Brittany told us as she reflected on the week. "You know, like you can't just *say* you trust Him. It really has to be real. You have to really believe that He'll do what He says He'll do. I'm going to really try to start doing that."

Really. I smiled at her pure, innocent, childlike faith. *If only I could have faith like that,* I thought to myself.

Indeed. Little did I realize how soon I would need "faith like that."

THE NEWS

On Monday afternoon, I was at my office when the phone rang. I picked up and said hello.

"Oh, honey! I'm so scared!" It was Nancy. All she could do was get out those words before breaking into sobs.

A chill went through me. I knew immediately what was wrong. At least I had a pretty good idea. She had gone for her quarterly visit to the doctor that afternoon, to hear the reports on her various scans. For a while I had accompanied her to those sessions. But they had become so stressful and filled with tension for both of us that finally she asked me to stop going. And so on that day she had gone alone. It was a mistake. Because on that day the news was not good.

"I'm so scared!" she kept saying over and over. "I'm so scared!"

"Let me come get you," I suggested.

"No, I'm okay to drive. But I can't go home. I don't want the girls to see me this upset." I knew right then that the reports had to be very bad to keep Nancy apart from her girls.

> I felt a sick ache of anxiety coursing through me. What was I about to hear?

"Well, what do you want to do?" I asked her, my mind spinning in search of options.

"I don't know," she said between sobs. "I just know I can't go home and have the girls see me like this. I don't want to frighten them."

"I'll tell you what," I suggested. "Why don't I meet you at the park across from the elementary school. We'll just meet there and talk for a little bit, until you feel better."

"Okay," she replied. There was no energy in her voice.

"Are you sure you can manage?" I pressed her.

"Yeah, I'm okay. I can drive."

We said good-bye, and I exhaled with a sigh as I put the phone down. "Lord, God, help me!" I prayed as I bent over with my head in my hands. I felt a sick ache of anxiety coursing through me. What was I about to hear? And what was getting ready to happen?

I closed up the office and got in the car and raced to the prearranged location. Nancy was waiting in her car. When I pulled up and got out, she got out and walked toward me. When I went to hug her, she just dissolved in tears. "Oh, honey! I'm going to die!" she blurted out. "I'm going to die!"

I helped her over to a picnic table, and we sat down. I just held her while she cried. Finally she was ready to talk. "The scans came back awful," she told me.

"Were the tumors enlarged?" I asked.

She was trying to nod and shake her head all at the same time. "They were slightly larger," she said, fighting back her tears, "but there were new sites. All over."

"What do you mean, all over?"

"In my liver. In my lungs. In my bone." She was choking on her sobs. Absolutely dissolving in grief. "Honey, I'm going to die!"

I held her for maybe ten minutes while she cried. Neither of us said anything. There was nothing to say. But it was a surreal moment. Sitting at a picnic table in the park, holding her—as if we were just two lovers enjoying a nice summer day. The sounds of children squealing with delight at the pool nearby. Cars quietly passing. A squirrel rooting around for nuts. A mommy pushing a stroller through the park. A plane buzzing overhead. The world all normal and active and alive and unaware. Unaware that my wife was staring death in the face.

And at a house down the street, three children waiting for their mother to come back. Not waiting by the door but waiting the way kids do: busy with playing or reading or doing something on the computer, but always aware that sooner or later the car is going to come down the alley and up into the driveway, and the person who gets out will be the person who never stops thinking about them, and that awareness of that person enables them to not worry about anything, because that person does all the worrying that's needed on their behalf.

"I don't know what to tell the girls," Nancy said after a while. "I don't want to have to tell them that their mother is dying."

"Well, you don't need to tell them you're dying," I replied.

"But I can't not tell them," she shot back.

"I didn't say not to tell them. But you don't know that you're dying. You just know that the cancer has spread."

She looked at me dubiously, as if to say, "What's the difference?"

"I don't think I can tell them," she said sadly. "I don't think I can get through it."

"That's okay. I'll tell them. I'll explain it to them."

"Oh, honey, would you?" she seemed relieved—or at least as relieved as a woman can feel who has just learned that her cancer has gone metastatic.

And so we finished up at the park, and it was now late in the afternoon, well past the time when Mommy would have been expected home. Nancy drove her car, and I followed her in mine.

We went inside together, and I did the thing I always hated having to do. "Brittany, can you come into the living room for a minute? Kristin, can you come out here? Amykins, come here, Mommy and Daddy want to talk to you." The girls dreaded those words, because they knew by then that whenever Daddy and Mommy called a meeting, it was usually to deliver bad news.

I know that many parents facing disease or tragedy choose not to tell their children much, if anything, about it. I personally think that's a huge mistake. Nancy and I decided from the very first day that she was diagnosed with cancer that we would tell our kids everything we knew (translated, of course, into terms they could understand). We never worried that they couldn't "handle" it, or that it would "upset" them. Of course it would upset them. But better to learn from an early age what life is really like—and what you're made of when you learn that—than to grow up into an adult and be blindsided by the shocking truth that the world is not always safe and life is not always fair, and, to make matters worse, to discover that your parents didn't bother to tell you that.

THE QUESTION

Nancy sat on the couch, Kristin to her right, Brittany to her left. Amy sat on my lap in the blue chair. Before I could even begin, Nancy started crying. Which, of course, brought expressions of alarm to the faces of the girls, who were already expecting bad news. Instinctively, Kristin threw her arms around her mother and hugged her tightly.

"Is it the scans, Mommy?" Brittany asked anxiously. She always did seem to get there first. "Did they not come out so well?"

Nancy broke down into sobs, nodding her head in agony.

"What did they say?"

"Girls," I began, trying to take control of the situation. "Mommy went to the doctor today and got her scans back.

They showed that some of the sites she's had are larger." I paused and swallowed. "They also showed that the cancer has spread. There are spots on her liver, bones, and lungs."

I was now choking up myself as I tried to get out the words. What tore it for me was the sight of Kristin, ten years old, looking up at her mother as if not believing what she was hearing, checking to see if Mommy was agreeing with what I was saying, and searching Mommy's face to see if she was going to be okay. As Nancy's tears fell, Kristin once again buried her face in her mother's hair and wrapped her arms around her tightly. She began crying too. Brittany enfolded Nancy from the other side. Seeing that, Amy bolted from my lap and joined the three of them on the couch.

> Nancy and I believed it would be far more cruel not to tell them the truth.

"Come here, Punkin," Nancy whispered as she took Amy up into her arms.

I had tears streaming down my face as I sat across from my family, Nancy and our three daughters, huddled together in a bond of love and sorrow. We all just cried for a while. It was probably the saddest moment in our home in all of the last ten years.

And as I knew it had to, the moment led to the inevitable question. I don't remember which of the girls asked the question, but after all the tears and sobs had gradually subsided into sniffles and coughs, one of them asked it.

"Mommy, are you going to die?"

I don't know how Nancy could have had more tears in her by that point in the day, but the question pierced her with yet deeper grief, and she sobbed as she held her babes tightly. I waited for a moment, to let the room quiet down. I myself was fighting to stay in control.

"Well," I began, my voice cracking, "we don't know that . . . it's, it's hard to say whether . . ." I stopped and took a deep breath. "Girls, none of us knows when Mommy's going to die. We know that the cancer has spread, and that makes it much, much more difficult for Mommy to stay alive. We're going to talk with the doctors about what they can do to fight the cancer, but . . . yes, there's a much stronger possibility now that Mommy might not live much longer."

I hated myself for having to say those words to my girls. Hated having to be the one to inflict such cruel, brutal truth on three children who, only minutes before, had been laughing and playing and imagining and creating and living their lives with joy. No wonder some parents choose not to tell. But there are no good options when the truth is that Mommy might die. It may feel—no, it *does* feel—unbelievably cruel to tell your children that terrible news. But Nancy and I believed it would be far more cruel not to tell them the truth. So I told them. But I still hated myself for having to do it.

Because I had to watch as one more time the four of them cried out their hearts.

"I don't want you to die, Mommy," Kristin was pleading.

This can't go on, I thought to myself. *This is too much. Oh, God, help us!* I remember crying out inside, feeling so helpless. And so alone. And so *not* connected to God.

As if to confirm that things had gone too far, Brittany suddenly dashed from the room. At first, I thought maybe she had gone for a Kleenex. But when she delayed, I started thinking, *Oh no, this has been too much for her. She's withdrawing into her room. I'd better go check on her.*

THE GIFT

But just as I was edging myself out of the chair, Brittany walked back into the room. She was surprisingly calm, relatively composed, and despite her tears was wearing a gentle, serene sort of smile. As soon as she came through the doorway, her eyes fastened on Nancy.

"Mommy," she said with a sniffle as she gently sat down on the couch, "I know that when people are dying, they sometimes want to go back and visit places that are special to them. And I know that you and Daddy liked New England a lot. And so I was thinking that maybe you'll want to go back there now. But I know it costs a lot of money to travel. So if you need it, I have my money from the trumpet fund that you can use to help you get there." And with that she held out an envelope to Nancy. It was the envelope for the trumpet fund. Stuffed with ones, fives, tens, twenties, and change. All $495 of it.

"Oh, Brittany!" Nancy exclaimed as she burst into tears. A sob broke from my mouth as well. Having no tears left to cry, we cried anyway. Our hearts were rended, just utterly overwhelmed by her offer.

Utterly overwhelmed, I submit, by lovingkindness. For that's what it was, of course. Pure lovingkindness! A passionate heart commitment to someone else's welfare, an almost irrational abandonment to their good, fueled by love and affection for the other person.

And now you can see why I have placed this story at the
end of the book. Because it says better than anything I know
how to say what God's lovingkindness looks
like in a fallen world where really bad stuff
happens. Isn't it just like God to show up in
our most extreme suffering? When our world
is falling apart, and our tears won't stop, and
we're out of words and practically out of our
mind, and the only thing we know to do is
the instinctive thing of crying out, with
scarcely a shred of faith even left to cry it:
"Oh, God, help us!"

> "I cannot take the pain away. But I will not leave you helpless in it."

Well, God showed up. In the worst moment of it all, God showed up. When I least
expected it but most needed it, God showed
up. God heard my prayer.

And, as He does 90 percent of the time when He shows
up, He showed up in the form of a person. In this case, a
thirteen-year-old girl who refused to shrink back from the
horror of terrible news but instead showed boldness in the
face of evil and went and laid hold of her most valuable treasure and brought it with an open hand to her suffering, desperate mother and, in a blow for all that is left of good in
this world, offered it without hesitation and without reservation, as if to say, "Here! Here is everything I have. Use it to
comfort some of your pain. I cannot take the pain away. But
I will not leave you helpless in it, Mommy. I am with you,
now and always."

That's God talking. No, not talking—*acting*. Showing
up. Being there for Nancy. And for me. And for my girls,

Brittany included. That's God incarnating His presence in a tough situation through a person whose heart was tender toward Him.

And isn't this story just a tiny retelling of the infinitely larger tale of how God has shown up for all of us in this desperate community we call the human race? Isn't it true that after evil entered the world through our own participation in it, God did not walk off and abandon us but climbed into this fallen world with us and went all the way to the worst depths to which evil subjects us?

And isn't it true that in order to do that He laid hold of *His* most valuable treasure and brought it with an open hand and offered it, without hesitation and without reservation, saying, "Here! Here is everything I have. I give it to you, and for you. It is the way out of your pain. I will not remove the pain right away. But I will not leave you helpless in it. I am with you, now and always"?

And isn't it true that He *is* with us always, even when we don't see Him or experience Him, and all we have left, if we can manage it, is trust? Because His lovingkindness *is* everlasting. It can never cease. He has abandoned His heart to us. His blood for our blood. His tears for our tears. His sorrow for our sorrow. His death for our death.

And His life for our life. Because His lovingkindness is everlasting. His lovingkindness can never die. His lovingkindness extends beyond the grave and into eternity. His lovingkindness is present and active right here, right now, because . . . *He's alive, you know!*

THE GIFT, PART 2

Plucked from the depths of despair by Brittany's selfless gesture, the five of us hugged and cried and prayed and finally realized that tears can make you hungry. But before we broke up the meeting to go get some dinner, Nancy and I assured Brittany that, as much as we appreciated her offer, she would not need to forfeit her trumpet money to fund any travel expenses.

Which meant that Brittany had exactly one week to come up with $150 if she was to reach her $645 goal. She wracked her brain to think up ways to make some quick money. Nothing beyond what she'd already tried came to mind. She called around for babysitting jobs. No one needed a babysitter.

Toward the end of the week, Brittany began resigning herself to the fact that the new trumpet would just have to wait until later in the summer, after she returned from band camp, and she could earn the rest of the money. So, having come to terms with that disappointment, she went to a movie on Friday afternoon with a friend.

While she was gone, God showed up for Brittany. I'm the only person in the world who knows all the pieces of this story. That puts me in a position to say quite confidently: God showed up for Brittany.

When Brittany came home from the movie, she said hi and went to her room. I already knew what was going to happen. So I was almost counting down the seconds: "Four, three, two, one . . . "

I heard her door fly open and then her footsteps rushing down the hall. "What's this?" she cried as she bolted into the kitchen. In her hand she held three crisp $50 bills. A look of utter amazement was glowing on her face. I myself had a knowing smile, but I just shrugged and played innocent.

"Where did this come from?" she asked incredulously. "Did you put this in my room?"

"No, Brittany."

"Then who did?"

I just shrugged. "It's amazing, isn't it?"

"Daddy, you know who did this! Why won't you tell me?"

Because I'm a man of many secrets. And I had sworn to the person who brought the money that I would never tell. So I didn't tell her, and never will. Because the gift-giver got more excitement out of surprising Brittany than anything else.

However, I'm not so sure that the gift-giver even knew that Brittany was saving up for a trumpet. And I know for a fact that the gift-giver had no way of knowing that earlier in the week Brittany had given up—at least in her own mind—all the money she had earmarked for the trumpet in order to do something good for her mother.

Nor did the gift-giver know that Brittany had been praying that week for a miracle. And I don't mean money for the trumpet. Yes, Brittany had been praying that the money would show up. But that wasn't the miracle she was asking for. She'd been praying for a miracle in regard to her mother. She was asking God for something—anything—some sign that He was with her and the family in our situation.

Well, when Brittany came back from Pine Cove and said that she was going to start trusting God about things in her life—and not just say it but actually do it, "really" do it—I think God took her seriously. Because I think she was serious. And so, just as He had used Brittany in such a powerful way to comfort her mother and father, I believe God favored Brittany with a miracle that was a true miracle on many counts.

Brittany certainly saw it that way. The next day she penned a letter to her anonymous benefactor and gave it to me with strict instructions to pass it on. I did. But of course I read it before doing so, and as I wiped the tears from my eyes after finishing it, I knew I had to make a copy. I'm glad I did, because now I can share it with you (with Brittany's permission):

June 13, 1998

To the Generous Person Who
Left $150 on My Bed Last Night:

Words cannot express my thanks to you for your wonderful gift. I had firmly set my mind on earning all $645 for my trumpet by today, and at the beginning of the week, I knew I needed a miracle to get what I wanted. You gave me a miracle. I am deeply thankful to you for your generosity.

Perhaps you may believe that you have given me three fifty-dollar bills. I see in that $150 much more. You have given me a trumpet, since the money I received will allow me to buy a brand new instrument and pay for tax. You have given me a reason to be happy in the face of my mother's health. I told a friend that I needed something incredibly good to happen to me this week, as I was terribly upset about my mother. You have brought some happiness into my life. Maybe most importantly, you gave me a lesson in giving. I was touched by your kindness and will try to do the same in years to come.

Every time I look at my new trumpet, which, I assure you, will be well loved and treated with great care, I will think of the unknown person who made it possible for me to get such a wonderful instrument. I will probably never get a name to go with that memory, but I feel that your anonymity has a greater impact on me than would your name.

Once again, I thank you for your gift. You cannot imagine my happiness as I came into my room and saw the money I needed sitting on my sheet music. At first I wondered if someone had really given the money to me; then I realized that so much cash is hard to leave laying around. I went out to thank my parents, whom I thought had given me that payment which I needed, and got one of the biggest shocks of my life. I hope that some day I can follow your example.

I have done my best to express my happiness and my gratefulness, but I still can't fully capture the feeling which overcame me last night. To whoever gave me that last $150, I thank you from the bottom of my heart.

Your grateful friend,
Brittany Hendricks

Who gave Brittany that last $150? Ultimately God did. God showed up for Brittany in the form of a generous person. So in a way, her letter, thanking her anonymous benefactor "from the bottom of my heart," is really a sort of thank-You to God from the bottom of her heart.

Where does one come by that kind of gratitude? By now, you know the answer. It's the sort of thing you acquire at the House of Mourning—if you are open to the wisdom of the place.

> It is better to go to a house of mourning
> Than to go to a house of feasting,
> Because that is the end of every man,
> And the living takes it to heart.[1]

Sigh!

Even now, after all of these words, I have a hard time telling you that it is "better" at the House of Mourning. Even I instinctively react, "How can one dare to say that?" Because I would never wish anyone to go there.

And yet—

And yet, having lived there for the past ten years, I cannot deny my own experience. It *has* been better for me at the House of Mourning. It really has. Hard to believe. Remarkable to find myself admitting it. But I have to say what I know to be true. I would not have chosen to go through anything I went through; but having gone through it, I would not trade it for all the world.

Yes, I have my loss. I always will. But look at what great comforts I have been given—yes, those simple but profound gifts that Ecclesiastes talks about. My girls. My work. My food. My health. My friends. My family. My faith. The gift of laughter. The gift of so many touching and vivid memories. So many memorable photographs. So much wonderful music. So many interesting books. The learnings of a lifetime. The wisdom yet to come. The rocks at Ogunquit. The sun that keeps coming up every morning. The full moon that still provokes love in my heart in the spring. The stars that lift my eyes upward into the night. The quiet of the dark, by now my friend.

And always—always and forever—the reassuring presence of the Mother Bunny. She came after me, just as she said. She'll never go away, even if others are taken away. And the confidence of that sets me free. Free to dream and have new adventures.

Goodnight stars
Goodnight air
Goodnight noises everywhere.[2]

Notes

Chapter 1: Intruder at the Party

1. Ecclesiastes 7:2.
2. Psalm 136:1.

Chapter 2: Love to the Extreme

1. 1 John 4:8, 16.
2. This kind of blood oath is not dissimilar to the covenant between David and Jonathan in 1 Samuel 20:11–17. Interestingly, the term *lovingkindness* is used twice in that passage (vv. 14–15). And the text says that Jonathan "loved [David] as he loved his own life." That's what *lovingkindness* means.
3. Margaret Wise Brown, *The Runaway Bunny,* illus. Clement Hurd (New York: Harper & Row, 1942).
4. An allusion to Psalm 107:23–24: "Those who go down to the sea in ships, who do business on great waters; they have seen the works of the LORD, and His wonders in the deep."
5. Lamentations 3:22–23.
6. Margaret Wise Brown, *Goodnight Moon,* illus. Clement Hurd (New York: Harper & Row, 1947).

Chapter 3: It's an Ugly Day in the Neighborhood

1. Someone will be quick to correct me by pointing out that Proverbs 1:7 says, "The fear of the LORD is the beginning of knowledge." I agree. That's why we began with the lovingkindess of God in the previous chapter.

2. Richard Morin, "Can We Believe in Polls About God?" *Washington Post,* 1 June, 1998.

3. Robert Wuthnow, "God Through American Eyes," *The Lutheran,* http://www.thelutheran.org/9612/page8.html.

4. "Most Americans Believe in Ghosts: Survey Shows 1/3 Accept Astrology, 1/4 Reincarnation," *WorldNetDaily, 27* February, 2003, http://www.worldnetdaily. com/news/article.asp?ARTICLE_ID=31266.

5. "Americans Draw Theological Beliefs from Diverse Points of View," *The Barna Group,* 8 October, 2002, http://www.barna.org.

Chapter 4: Life: Why Bother?

1. I would caution the reader that there are almost as many interpretations of Ecclesiastes as there are books on Ecclesiastes. In my opinion, the person who "cracked the code" on understanding the book was a Roman Catholic scholar in the 1960s named Addison Wright. He made a very convincing case that the key to interpreting Ecclesiastes is to recognize its structure, which the Hebrew text reveals through the repetition of key phrases. If you're thinking of exploring Ecclesiastes more deeply, I encourage you to seek out Wright's article. Addison G. Wright, "The Riddle of the Sphinx: The Structure of the Book of Qoheleth," *Catholic Biblical Quarterly* 30 (1968), 313–34, http://studentorg.cua.edu/cbib/CBQ.cfm.

2. Ecclesiastes 1:2.

3. Ecclesiastes 2:24–26; 3:12–13, 22; 5:18–20; 8:15.

4. Ecclesiastes 5:18.

5. Ecclesiastes 9:9.

Chapter 5: The Glacier

1. Romans 8:1.

2. Romans 8:38–39.

3. See C. S. Lewis, *A Grief Observed: With an Afterword by Chad Walsh* (New York: Bantam Books, 1976), 136–49.

4. C. S. Lewis, *Mere Christianity* (New York: Macmillan, 1943), 123.

5. Lewis, *A Grief Observed,* 5.

6. Ibid., 4–5.

7. Job 2:13.

8. Romans 8:20–23.

9. The Greek word used in Romans 8:20 is *mataiotes,* meaning "emptiness," "vanity," or "futility." The word conveys a very similar idea as the Hebrew word *hebel.*

Chapter 6: "Where Are You?"

1. Brown, *Runaway Bunny.*

2. I have mostly given examples from my own American culture, a Judeo-Christian culture at that. But I don't mean to limit the question, where is God? to Americans. The sense of abandonment by God in the midst of pain and suffering is a universal condition, shared even by cultures that believe in a very different God than I do.

3. Genesis 3:9.

4. I write this paragraph knowing that it will cause pain for some readers whose mothers were or are anything but devoted and committed. I grieve with anyone in that situation. But the failures of our human mothers only reinforce my point. I am talking about God here. God is the "Mommy" who never leaves us or forsakes us. God is the One whose lovingkindness is everlasting. In that way, God shows us characteristics that are ideally part of motherhood. As for human mothers, their lovingkindness can never measure up to God's. Their mothering may be praiseworthy (at times) because it is like His, or it may be blameworthy (at times) because it is very unlike His. The hope is that a mother's lovingkindness is lasting; it can never be *ever*lasting.

Chapter 7: How Sunday School Saved My Life

1. See 1 Samuel 17:41–43.

Chapter 8: "Come Forth!"

1. John 11:35. Technically speaking, this is the shortest verse in the English Bible. First Thessalonians 5:16 is the shortest verse in the Greek New Testament.

2. John 11:3

3. John 11:21, 32. Some conjecture that Mary's question was asked in a different spirit than Martha's. According to that interpretation, Martha may have evidenced mistrust, but Mary's (identical) question was actually a statement of trust. I think there's probably truth to that. But even if Mary was, in effect, saying, "Lord, I have confidence that if You had been here, You have

the power to heal my brother and You would have kept him from dying," the implication of the question is evident: "You were *not* here, and my brother is dead as a result." The feeling of disappointment, if not betrayal, is overwhelming. No wonder Jesus broke down and wept (v. 35).

4. John 11:32–33

5. John 11:33

6. John 14:14 (the same word is used). See also Luke 24:38.

7. Philippians 2:5–8

8. Maybe that was because Jesus had just come from declaring, "I am the Son of God" (John 10:36). Martha took great care to assure Him that she was in line with that: "I have believed that You are the Christ, the Son of God" (John 11:27). Meanwhile the crowd, too, was thinking about Jesus's miracles (John 11:37).

9. John 11:37

10. Genesis 2:17

11. I am well aware of the special cases of Enoch, Moses, and Elijah, as well as the doctrine of "translation" in 1 Thessalonians 4:13–18. But those matters go beyond the purpose of this book, so I won't deal with them here. (By the way, some people, like Lazarus, had to die twice!)

12. John 11:43

13. John 11:44

14. Romans 8:11

Chapter 9: The Power of Presence

1. I probably will get Skip in trouble with some by mentioning this visit, because I doubt that in a large church like ours (6,000 members) a senior pastor could possibly make hospital and hospice visits to each and every parishioner and their loved ones—or else it would be his full-time job! But that doesn't mean some people don't place that expectation on him.

2. 1 Corinthians 12:26.

Chapter 10: God Shows Up

1. Ecclesiastes 7:2.

2. Brown, *Goodnight Moon*.

We hope you enjoyed this product from
Northfield Publishing. Our goal at Northfield
is to provide high quality, thought provoking
and practical books and products that connect
truth to the real needs and challenges of
people like you living in our rapidly changing
world. For more information on other books
and products written and produced from a
biblical perspective write to:

Northfield Publishing
215 West Locust Street
Chicago, IL 60610